Miraculous Journeys of a Mundane Man:

Illustrated True Stories of Other Lives, Other Worlds, and Visionary Travel

American Tao Series, Book Four

S. Strasnick, PhD

Illustrated by D. Moll, L.Ac.

Mystic Tao
Publishing

ISBN-13: 978-0-9976471-3-6
ISBN-10: 0-9976471-3-2

Cover Art & Book Design:
Steven Strasnick

Illustrations:
Diana Moll

Special thanks to my wife Katie, without whom none of this book could have been written, and to Diana Moll for her inspiring artwork

Printed in the United States of America

Mystic Tao Publishing
themysticnerd@icloud.com
Santa Cruz, CA

Miraculous Journeys of a Mundane Man:

Illustrated True Stories of Other Lives, Other Worlds, and Visionary Travel

An American Tao Book

The Tibetan Book of the Dead, Dante's *Divine Comedy*, Lewis Carroll's *Alice in Wonderland*, C. G. Jung's *Red Book*, Sri Aurobindo's *Savitri*, and Carlos Castaneda's *Tales of Power*, to name a few, are examples of extraordinary works describing the Soul's journey through mystical worlds of vision, both real and imagined.

While *Miraculous Journeys of a Mundane Man* is not yet counted among these distinguished tomes, like them it intrepidly dares to explore previously untraveled ground. It tells the true story of what happened when a skeptical, spiritual neophyte sat down to begin a daily practice of meditation and somehow slid through a crack between worlds, ultimately ending up in a strange new psychic dimension of the Multi-Soul.

In repeated visits over an extended period, the author, very much a mundane man, experienced a plethora of strange visions and apparitions. These led him on a journey across multiple realms and worlds, ultimately taking him into the celestial chambers of a mysterious white-bearded being, where final secrets were revealed, before returning him to earth, transfigured. The narrative chronicle of the author's journey is presented in this volume, beautifully illustrated by the whimsical drawings of the gifted artist, Diana Moll.

Some Words to Ponder

"Why, sometimes I've believed as many as
six impossible things before breakfast."

--- The White Queen to Alice
in Lewis Carroll's
Through the Looking Glass ... (1871)

"And remember, no matter
where you go, there you are."

-- Buckaroo Banzai, in the movie
"The Adventures of Buckaroo Banzai" (1984),
also sometimes attributed to Confucius

"The sole purpose of life has been
to pass on what was learned."

--Professor Norman in the movie "Lucy" (2014)

"The undiscovered country from whose bourn
No traveler returns, puzzles the will"

-- Hamlet in Shakespeare's *Hamlet*

"Death is just the turning of a key in a lock."

-- James Delaney in the FX Networks
TV Series "Taboo," (2017) S01E08

"A frog in a well knows nothing of the great ocean."

-- An ancient Chinese idiom

About the Author, In His Own Words
The Story of an Errant Seeker

In the past I have worked as a professional philosopher, a software developer, a computer animator, and a research scientist. It seems as if I have spent my whole life studying and learning. I am over-educated and over-degreed, and very much a nerd, big-brained and socially awkward. I'm addicted to doing the daily Sudoku, taking spin class, and practicing kung fu. How and why I ended here, consumed with writing about mystical experiences, remains the great mystery of my life.

Special thanks again to Diana for agreeing to travel down the rabbit hole with me and put pen to paper to bring my journeys to life.

About the Illustrator, In Her Own Words
The Story of an Errant Artist

Former Record store clerk with a degree in art throws over graphic design for Chinese medicine. Never really stops drawing. Never really stops looking for a niche. Realizes drawing is not a niche, but it is possible to draw a niche in which to rest for a moment or two.

Thanks to Steve for asking me to draw his journey. It is a privilege to walk through someone's personal world. A traveler cannot help but to emerge changed, perhaps in unexpected ways. I hope that my attempts to picture this journey will help you, Dear Reader, along you way. If not, please, feel free to draw your own postcards home.

About the Artwork

All illustrations were done in pen and ink by Diana Moll. Some of these were further edited in Photoshop by the author in order to add texture effects, additional foreground or background, and/or to resize or reposition certain elements. These include parts of the drawings for visions numbered 8, 9, 19, 20, 21, 23, 25, 28, 31, 32, 33, 34, 35, 37, 44, and 50. In all these cases, although Diana's work was the starting point for the image, she bears no responsibility for any damage inadvertently done by me to the integrity of her vision.

Table of Contents

Introduction

On December 27th, 2014 I sat down to begin what I hoped would become a daily practice of meditation, not suspecting that my world was about to irrevocably change. Within minutes of closing my eyes I witnessed the first of many strange visions and apparitions that would visit me over the next year and a half, the vast majority occurring within the first three months before starting to diminish in frequency. I had somehow opened the floodgates to the worlds of my unconscious.

At first, surprisingly, I did not consider these experiences unusual or deserving of further study. Like you, I've learned to accept my nighttime dreams as a normal part of life. These just seemed a kind of daytime dream. If anything, I found them entertaining. I simply assumed that they, like dreams, were something that happened when you slipped into an alternative state of consciousness, something best experienced and then quickly forgotten. After all, that was the advice offered by all the introductory books on meditation at which I looked.

Over the next couple of months, as these experiences continued to accumulate, my perspective started to change. My curiosity began to grow. Was what was happening to me typical? I talked to many long-term meditators and asked them about their experiences. I dove into the mystical literature to see if I could discover historical antecedents to my experiences. While none of the people I talked to reported anything remotely similar, I did find examples in history of mystics who had.

Things grew even stranger for me on March 24th, 2015. On that day approximately 45 minutes into my meditation session, I experienced what I subsequently refer to in this book as "The Descent." Several things occurred simultaneously. It began with my awareness suddenly snapping back into the ordinary world from whatever kind of trance state I had been in. The first thing I noticed was that the CD player in my room that had been playing soft meditation music was now skipping wildly, like the old fashioned phonograph, repeatedly jumping back to the same spot, in an endless loop. The volume seemed much louder as well. I thought the room was shaking. My body definitely was.

As more physical sensations returned to me, I realized that I had been hyperventilating, breathing dramatically quicker than I normally did during meditation. More significantly, I felt a torrent of energy streaming into the top of my head and down my spine, where it seemed to settle in my lower abdominal region, below my navel. I did not experience this energy as painful, though it was certainly intense. Words don't really suffice, but the best way to describe it was to call it a physical experience of ecstatic bliss.

In my readings I had learned about the phenomenon of the Kundalini experience, in which energy reportedly shot up the practitioner's spine. This seemed like a variant of that experience, a kind of reverse Kundalini. The physical aftershocks from this experience reverberated through my meditation sessions for the next week. The psychic aftershocks, which carried over into my everyday life, lasted much longer.

Since that event, I have often calmed myself with the thought that I knew "why the Buddha smiled." At times I considered that this phrase would make a good title for the account I soon felt compelled to write. Because of that event and others that followed it, I finally accepted both the uniqueness and the strangeness of what was happening to me. The rationalist in me felt the accumulated body of all these experiences deserved further study and documentation. The books of the American Tao series were the result.

While the first three books in the series, *Meditation's Secret Treasure*, *Hidden Teachings of the Mystic I-Ching*, and *Many Lives, Many Worlds*, engaged in serious philosophical and psychological inquiry into the meaning of my visions, my goal for this one is much simpler. I wish for my visions to now speak for themselves, with minimal commentary or analysis added by me.

To my short description of each vision, I add only its associated I-Ching name (in quotes) and a quartile-based representation of its relative spiritual power (via 1,2,3, or 4 Δ's, with ΔΔΔΔ the most powerful). Readers wishing to delve deeper into these latter topics can refer to the previous books *Hidden Teachings of the Mystic I-Ching* and/or *Many Lives, Many Worlds*. Those interested in the nature of my meditational practice and the Taoist philosophy behind it should see *Meditation's Secret Treasure*.

Because my spiritual experiences came to me in such a rich and vivid visual manner, my words can only go so far in conveying their nature. To help tell their stories, I have asked the very talented artist Diana Moll to provide an illustration for each of them. I know from my previous interactions with her that not only is Diana an accomplished visual artist, but she is also an experienced traveler within the spiritual realms as well as an accomplished practitioner of Chinese medicine and kung fu.

I presented Diana only with the written descriptions of the visions and asked her to draw what she experienced as she read them. I didn't tell her what scenes within the visions to portray or what elements I felt should be highlighted in the subsequent illustration. In fact, I gave her the most minimal of artistic direction, wanting her own distinctive visual style to emerge unfiltered by my expectations. I was both surprised and delighted to see how well she captured the inner truth of what I had experienced.

When I began the task of telling my story, I was skeptical about the possible reality of spiritual worlds and the continuation of some form of life after death. The existence of a soul independent of the body seemed highly unlikely; I believed consciousness resided in the brain and would die when the heart stopped beating. The concept of reincarnation seemed nothing more than a meaningless fable invented by humanity to quell their fear of death.

The sheer weight of my visions as well as the act of writing about them undermined my most strongly held views about reality and exposed the fundamental fragility of my beliefs. I know now that the world is a much larger and grander place than I ever could have imagined. So too is the nature of the true self, which, though once hidden, has been vividly revealed to me as a multidimensional being (the Multi-Soul) engaged in an eons long, epic journey of evolution and redemption.

Though the soul's ultimate liberation may be countless lifetimes away, the fact of its inevitability brings with it a profound spiritual liberation that illuminates the meaning of our lives in the here and now.

The Illustrator's Process

(In her own words)

Step one: read the text; find an image that feels doable; draw a pencil sketch.

Step two: ink in the very barest, minimal indications of shapes and erase the pencil. Eat more breakfast.

Step three: Slap on so ink wash. Don't worry that it looks liked you totally f@#ked up the whole thing. Splash away the inner critic.

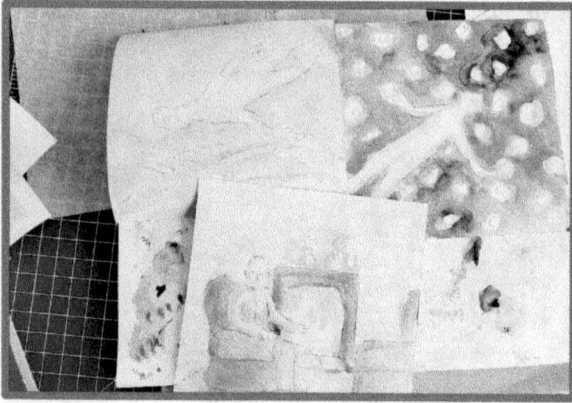

Step four: Refer to text to be sure of important bits. Use the pen. F@#k it up. Make it better. Notice the mess up actually looks good. Riff on that. Add some more ink wash. Ask the drawing what it wants. Consider starting over. Scratch away looking for some truth. Then, almost suddenly the drawing says OK that's it. Scan it and send to writer. Have an ice cream sandwich.

Down the Rabbit Hole

"It's all just a bunch of New Age
mumble jumble and fairy tale nonsense
until you open your eyes and suddenly find that you have
disappeared and are now
a teenage boy, who, as a
rebellious member of a primitive tribe,
is trekking through an alien jungle
with a bunch of his pals,
unwittingly on the way
to an encounter with
a mythical monster,
an angry mother,
and a new found destiny."
"That will get your
attention."

And So It Begins

Once upon a time a rather mundane man (aka the author) sat down to begin a simple practice of meditation. After all, everyone was doing it. What harm could come from it? Mindfulness was all the rage, and much was being written about its health and stress relieving benefits. It was true that he entered into this exercise with somewhat different motives than most, having been bitten at an early age by the philosophy bug, but meditation was meditation. He was a little curious about what might happen, but he was also innately skeptical about all things religious or otherworldly.

His approach was simple. He would sit normally in a soft, overstuffed leather chair in his upstairs bedroom with the windows blocked to seal out as much light as possible. He set an alarm for 30 minutes. To help dampen the impact of background noise, he played "New Age," ambient music on an Internet music station in another room. He sat naturally with his arms resting on his upper thighs, cupped his hands, closed his eyes, and breathed normally. He focused on the dark grainy field displayed on the back of his closed eyelids.

That was it, nothing fancy, no guided meditation, no counting breaths, no chanting mantras. Just gazing into the formless darkness before his closed eyes. But then something completely unexpected happened. Within a few minutes he fell into an empty black void in which a black and white photograph of an unknown young man appeared. Soon after that he found himself back in his room being observed by two individuals who were pulling up chairs to get closer to him. And then he noticed that the lights were on, which they weren't, and that little bit of cognitive dissonance snapped him back to reality.

So began the mundane man's travels. For the first couple of weeks all of his visions took place indoors, as if he was not yet comfortable enough with his visionary travels to stray far from home. He was apparently suffering from a form of visionary agoraphobia. In fact, for the first week, his visions never let him out of his room.

It wasn't until halfway through the second week that he was able to go downstairs to his kitchen and look out a window. When he did finally leave the house, it was only to immediately go back inside an imaginary yoga studio, where he met the female Teacher figure who would accompany him on so many of his subsequent travels. A full account of these preparatory visions can be found in the first and third books of the *American Tao* series, *Meditation's Secret Treasure* and *Many Lives, Many Worlds*.

With the Teacher's blessing and his visionary agoraphobia cured, he was now ready to begin his travels into the wider realms of the mystical worlds, having completed the initiation and orientation components of his journey. These are the travels that will be presented in the following pages, organized into narratives that will document his visits to the different visionary realms of the three mystical world levels, so vividly described in the Shamanic tradition.

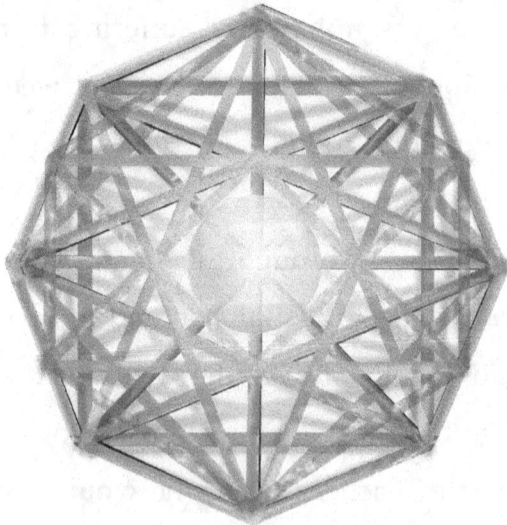

Major Personas within the Visions

- *The Seeker*: the author when present in the mundane world and during the initial stages of meditation

- *The Witness*: the author involved in a vision only as a passive, non-embodied observer and not engaged within the vision as a participant

- *The Traveller*: the author as an active participant in the vision as a version of himself, usually as a 35-year old. Also the general name for the author's persona in his visionary odyssey. (Note the British spelling for "traveller" to indicate the special nature of visionary travel)

- *The Rider*: the author when he occupies the body of a non-human entity who is a participant within the vision, such as the Dragon

- *The Other-Self*: the character of the author seen in a vision when sitting in meditation as the Seeker

- *The Teacher*: the wise woman who guides and instructs the Traveller in his journey's through the visions

- *The First Son*: the first born, teenage son of his jungle tribe's chief (his father) and queen shaman (his mother)

- *The Spirit Walker*: the ceremonial name for First Son's mother, the tribe's shaman, who possesses psychic powers

- *The Apprentice Blacksmith*: the young, peasant apprentice who is a member of the Watchers, who serve as lookouts for their village, and is conscripted into the King's service

- *The King*: the ruler of the castle that includes the apprentice's village in his domain

- *The Shadow Warrior*: the champion of the Dark Army that is arrayed against the King and whom the apprentice must challenge

- *The Adept*: one of a series of cloned youths who are in training to be elevated into the Dragon Clan and prepared for entry into the sacred Pyramid

- *The Journeyman*: the Adept, newly elevated, who, having passed selection rituals, begins his exploration inside the Pyramid

- *The Magister*: the head of the Council of Elders who awaits the Traveller's completion of his journey and full integration.

With the exception of the Teacher, the King, the Shadow Warrior, and the Magister, the mundane man assumed the identity of all these different personas within his visions, seeing through their eyes, living their lives, thinking their thoughts.

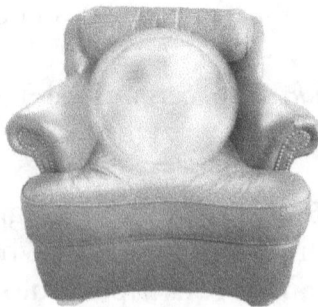

List of Narratives

The Journey

The complete account of the sixty four visions,
presented in narrative order,
with accompanying illustrations

The "Nexus Formation" Narrative:

The Traveller, having left home and now ready to begin his
journey through the mystic worlds, witnesses a symbolic
depiction of the process of spiritual alchemy,
in which Heavenly energies descend to merge
with Earth energies and then are refined
in an evolving process of transformation,
leading to a new door:
the purifying Wall of Flame

ELEMENTAL DOMAIN:

WIND

On the Wings of
Gathering and Dissolution

1. The Wings of Flight
"Observing"

The Rider

Thick foliage and low hanging willow branches surround the Rider in his backyard. He is watching a bird in flight. The bird glides over the creek, with sharply pointed wings held at an acute angle. The leading edge of the underside of the wings is a dark, greyish blue, while the bottom edge is reddish brown. Suddenly, he is no longer standing in his backyard looking up at the bird. Instead, he finds himself quickly rising up through the tree branches. He is flying. Has he become the very bird he was watching? The Rider is soon far above what should have been his neighborhood, but wasn't. Arrayed below him are brightly colored rows of small cottages made up of stucco-like cob material. The roofs are a thatched material, darker but also colored. There are dirt and gravel roads winding among the rows of cottages. The Rider feels that this is his territory. Even though he is flying and suspended beneath two large wings, he soon realizes he is not a bird. His head is perched on a long neck, his body smooth and featherless, and he has two legs and arms tucked beneath him. In spite of his present state, he recognizes the objects below him as human houses and roads. The Rider soon is flying much closer to the ground, traveling up a steep hill over a dirt road just above the roofs of the cottages lining the road to his right. He climbs a hill very much like the one in his neighborhood. It ends at a forested area, with meadows and groves of redwood and oak trees and footpaths leading into its interior.

∆∆

2. The Spirit Condensation
"Great Accumulation"

The Traveller

The Traveller walks on a dirt path surrounded by oaks and pines and some scattered redwood trees. Heavy underbrush lines the sides of the path. The sky is a bright blue. No other persons or animals are visible. As he comes around a corner curving to the left, he sees a sharply sloping drop-off to his right overlooking grassy meadows visible a few hillsides below. Sunlight streams through the trees dappling the path. As he looks to the open area on his right, he sees a shower of whitish fuzzy particles beginning to drift down from the otherwise clear blue sky. Wave after wave of these translucent flakes slowly drift down from above. There are neither clouds visible nor any perceptible currents of wind. Even though the air is warm and still, he feels like he is in the midst of a flurry of ephemeral snowflakes. It is as if a field of dandelions strewn across some heavenly alpine meadow has decided to give up its seeds in one prolific burst. None of these particles accumulate on the ground, nor did any seem to fall on him, in spite of the fact that they are tumbling and drifting all around him. He thinks to himself that this must be what it is like to dodge raindrops, albeit slow and lazy ones. Whatever these objects are, they seem to disappear when they get close to him or to the ground.

Δ

3. The Children's Pilgrimage
"Following"

The Traveller

The Traveller is located to the left of a hiking path in a clearing in the woods. The clearing is roughly oval in shape, with grasses and small bushes in it. The path, which is lined with trees, curves around the clearing. He is not alone. Next to him is the Teacher, who indicates that she is in control of the events he is seeing. A seemingly endless procession of children of various ages and sizes, both boys and girls, come down the path towards him. They are dressed in a wide variety of attire, displaying many different colors and textures. They disappear as they walk past him, rounding the bend. The lines of children are shepherded by young adults, who, standing by the sides of the path, guide them on their way. The path is wide enough for three children to walk alongside each other, forming loose rows of three abreast. Their pace, as well as their demeanor, is relaxed and carefree, with some children sometimes walking a little slower or faster than others, not always in a straight line. As a result, though their relative positions within the progression are not always fixed, the rows would periodically re-form until the next shuffling occurred. To the Traveller, the pilgrimage looks like a flowing river of vibrant humanity, whose areas of ebbs and flows correspond to the jostling and intermingling movements of the children.

ΔΔΔΔ

4. A Melding of Souls
"Gathering"

The Traveller

The Traveller is standing in a clearing in the woods. He watches as rows of children flow past him around a bend on a hiking path and then move away. The width of the path is narrow, only wide enough for one person at a time to walk along it. As the scene comes more into focus, he realizes something strange is occurring. As the children round the corner, their growth suddenly accelerates, and they rapidly age before his eyes, from child to adult, from adult to elder. Some grow at different speeds than others. At the same time as they age, the solidity and opacity of their bodies start to diminish and fade away. The faster they age, the more translucent their bodies become, until they are almost completely transparent, ghostlike in appearance. Shifting his gaze behind him to get a better look at this phenomenon, he sees the path abruptly stop. At the end of the path stands a large translucent figure, the Nexus. Its form, continually fluctuating in shape, is hard for him to focus on. As the transparent body of each individual gets close to the Nexus, it swells and reaches out to grab the walker, like the pseudopod of an amoeba reaching out for its prey. The shape of the walker distorts as well, as it is pulled in. The shape of the Nexus temporarily morphs into the shape of the body it absorbs, before resuming its amorphous shape, cycling from one consumed shape to another, as an endless stream of figures dissolve into its figure-shaped vortex of pulsating energy.

△△△△

5. The Spirit Migration
"Great Harvest"

The Traveller

The Traveller is walking through a redwood and oak forest along a dirt-covered hiking trail. The trail is set in a small depression next to an upward sloping hillside on the left and a downward slope on the right. Trees line both sides, which is thick with brush and grasses and ferns. The walk proceeds uneventfully until he perceives what feels like a shift in atmospheric pressure. The leaves of the trees and the grasses and ferns begin to rustle, even though there is no apparent wind. At this moment he is engulfed on all sides by a sea of small, translucence, glistening objects floating upwards into the sky. He looks for their place of origin but finds none. They are not coming out of the ground, but rather seem to be just materializing out of thin air, already in motion. These objects are about the size and shape of a hand with fingers cupped together, pointed upwards, like an upside down jellyfish. Like a jellyfish, they have a pearly, incandescent, shimmering color to them, lit by glowing, internal, luminous phosphorescence. They shimmer like thousands of sparkling flames as they rise into the air, row after row ascending in a seemingly endless progression into the heavens.

Δ

6. The Fiery Gauntlet
"The Cauldron"

The Seeker

The Seeker is sitting in his room, meditating. He is in the transitional phase of meditation, his body numb and his breathing slow and gentle. Sinking deeper into trance, he is still aware of himself and his situation. A flat two-dimensional image of a series of four pine trees sitting on a ridge slowly comes into focus. The four trees are spaced equally apart, spread out just enough that no tree overlaps with the branches of its neighbors. The trees are a rich, highly saturated forest green in color. The sky behind them appears whitish grey. There are no visible shadows in the scene. Initially the scene is completely static. Nothing is moving. The air is still. Soon the air around the trees begins to shimmer and vibrate. The flickering air around the trees starts to glow a bright translucent green, completely enveloping the branches and foliage of the trees. The trees are still visible through the bright glare of these dancing flame-shaped phantasms. The trees are on fire, but they are not being consumed. There is no smoke. The flames are not the normal yellow orange red of a burning tree, but are a semi-transparent, bright shade of chartreuse green. Suddenly the view zooms towards the flaming trees, which take up more and more of the image. Soon, passing through the branches of a tree, only the flames themselves are visible. Then the scene transforms again. All that remains is a solid expanse of bright translucent chartreus.

Δ

The "Face of the Deep" Narrative:

Having been purified by fire, the Traveller witnesses a
symbolic depiction of the process of spiritual baptism,
in which Spirit energies penetrate the dark waters of the Soul,
illuminating her realm with their golden rays,
leading to a new door:
Spirit's golden light
reflected back onto itself

ELEMENTAL DOMAIN:
LAKE

At Play in the Radiant Depths

7. Hovering over Stormy Seas

"Dispersing"

The Rider

The Rider sees dark, broiling clouds sweeping across a troubled sky. Below him an angry sea throbs and thrashes. The Rider is suspended in the midst of this boiling cauldron, buffeted by heavy winds and blowing foam. Only his large wingspan keeps him airborne, as he hovers unsteadily above the waters. He feels his head held aloft on a long muscled neck and body, his four legs hugged tightly to his sides, his tail trying to keep him balanced. He knows himself as the Dragon. The ocean rises up before him at a 45-degree angle. The seas are slate blue with the darkest elements almost black. The waves are not rounded or rolling. There are no curves to be seen. Instead, jagged edges are all he sees, the waves like the teeth of some ravenous maw trying to consume him and the blowing foam the frothing saliva of some rabid beast. The waves lash out towards him, trying to pull him into the dark depths below. In spite of the elemental violence of his surroundings, he feels no fear or peril or any emotion at all. He doesn't know why he is here, but he still tries to take in as many details as he can. At this point he feels himself pulled toward the surface of the slashing waves. He goes into a steep dive, waves growing closer and closer as he plummets downwards in a tight spiral.

Δ

8. Swimming in Heaven's Light
"Abundance"

The Rider

The Rider is deep under the sea. The waters are warm and welcoming, caressed by slow moving tropical currents. Although he is far below the surface, the waters are translucent and clear, illuminated by shafts of shimmering light penetrating into their depths. The glistening image of the sun, though suspended high in the heavens, floats as a fuzzy sphere on its surface. The waters reflect the colors of the warm sunlit sky and are a luminous greenish blue. Softly undulating wave-like mounds roll across its surface. The Rider realizes that he is in the body of sea creature, with a long body and neck, and wings on its back that propel it through the waters and a tail that it uses to steer. He rejoices in his newly found freedom, swimming and frolicking, making loops and figure eights in the receptive waters. Even though submerged, he feels as if he is flying. His movements express the joy and freedom he is experiencing. He feels content and perfectly at home as he slices and darts up and down and left and right through the waters. He has no thoughts or memories but only the pure joy brought on by swimming. Ultimately, he begins a set of lazy spirals that take him deeper and deeper into the warm soothing depths.

ΔΔΔ

9. Golden Light Reflections
"Seeking Harmony"

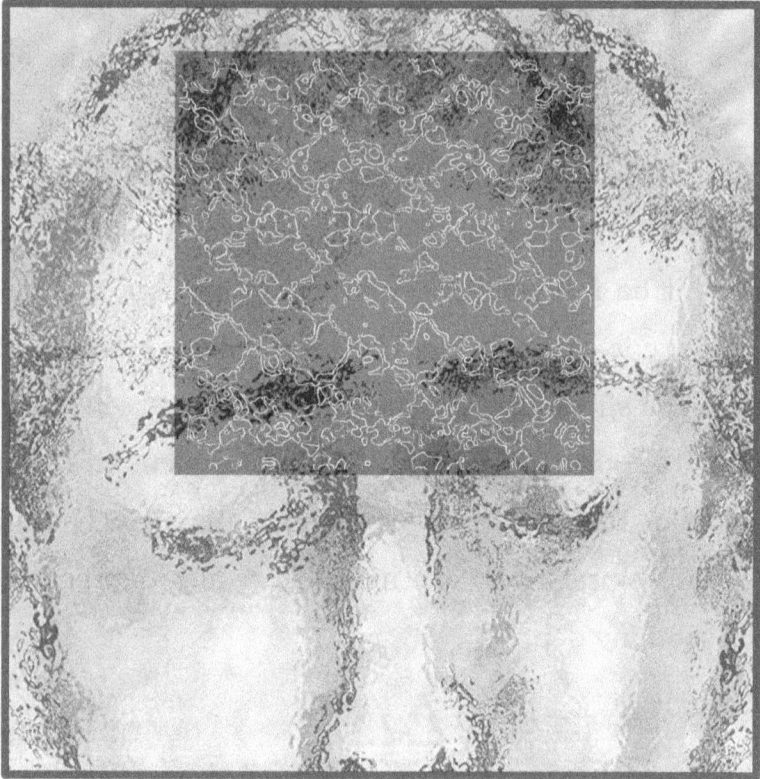

The Seeker

The Seeker, sitting in trance, sees a colorless, empty expanse, neither black nor white. Soon, a perfectly square window begins to take shape in the center of his vision. He sees only the square. The space around it is now invisible. Within the window, a brightly colored field of azure blue appears. The image is not that of an unmoving, solid shape, however, but more like the fluid-like surface of a watery volume. Horizontal rows of waves cover the field's surface. Each row is made up of a series of repeating segments of identical, polygonally shaped facets, like so many diamond shaped teeth. He recognizes these shapes as the result of some kind of wind-blown choppiness. As the image comes into further focus, it begins to move. The waves with their pyramid shaped clusters of chop slowly undulate across the watery surface, flowing from the bottom of the image to the top, at a gradual, constant pace. At the diamond shaped tip of each of the choppy wave segments, a bright golden light glistens and sparkles, reflections from an unseen sun in the skies above it. After a short interval, the blue background begins to get darker and darker, going from blue to purple to black. Soon, all that remains is a field of sparkling golden stars in a black night sky.

ΔΔΔΔ

The "Dragon Encounter" Narrative:

Leaving the Surface World to descend into the Under World,
the Traveller becomes First Son, a member of a tribal people
living in a primitive jungle realm,
on an odyssey to confront the great Dragon
and to learn his destiny
from his mother, the Spirit Walker,
leading him to a new door: a choice
between two paths in the Well of Souls,
one up, the other down

ELEMENTAL DOMAIN:
THUNDER

The Sleeper Rises from its Slumbers

10. Golden Light Descends
"Concealed Brilliance"

The Witness

The Witness is buried beneath the earth, with nothing visible on any side except for roots, dirt, and stones. He is moving in a downward direction, with his orientation fixed straight ahead. Around him everything is totally black except for an illuminated area in the center of his vision. The lit area is circular in shape with edges fading off slowly into darkness, curving around him as it follows him down. He does not feel that he is moving through a hole or tunnel in the ground. Instead, the ground seems liquid-like as he sinks through it, his substance having lost all corporeality. Moving deeper, he is no longer surrounded by earth or stones. Instead, he is immersed within a thick tangle of vertical tree roots of varying thicknesses, ranging from several inches in width to some only as wide as a piece of string. Many of the larger roots wind continuously around each other in helical shapes similar to that of DNA. When the light passes over the dull brown roots, they are illuminated in a rich golden glow. The clumps of earth and various sized stones and debris amidst the roots are similarly transformed. Occasionally, metallic rocks reflect this light back. His awareness is enshrined in this golden orb of light. No other color is visible except for the pale brown hues on the periphery of the light and the golden hues ablaze in its center.

ΔΔΔ

11. In Search of the Mystery
"Approaching"

The First Son

The First Son walks on a dirt path surrounded by a lush tropical jungle. The sunlight is dappled due to its passage through the thick canopy above and somewhat diminished by the edges of the surrounding cliffs. Following behind him is a group of dark skinned, shorthaired boys dressed in little more than loincloths wrapped around their waists. The older boys wear beaded neckpieces. Similarly dressed, his neckpiece is larger and more ornamental. They all look to him for leadership. They move fairly briskly along the downward sloping path, on the way to the low-lying swamp at the edge of the forest to investigate the rumors of a sighting of some strange crocodile-like beast. He had been forbidden to go there by his mother, the tribe's Spirit Walker and Queen, and the War Chief, his father, because it would be too dangerous. He doesn't understand the fuss. After jogging at an easy pace for a while, the group nears the swamp. They feel no sense of apprehension. This swamp forms during the rainy season when the Great River overflows its banks. The path grows soft and muddy. The jungle grows brighter as more light from the sun penetrates the canopy thinned by frequent flooding. Looking ahead they see the beginnings of the swamp in the distance. They peer over the still waters looking for any signs of life. Aside from some gently approaching wavelets at the far edge of the swamp, they spy nothing out of the ordinary.

ΔΔ

12. The Dragon in the Swamp
"Waiting"

The First Son

First Son and his young friends stand at the edge of the swamp, waiting to catch a glimpse of an old crocodile rumored to have come to their jungle. They are on a hunting trail, surrounded on each side by thick tropical jungle growth and towering trees. Scanning the water's edge, they spy two red eyes peering at them from the swamp. Soon thereafter, the rest of a green reptilian head emerges, glaring hungrily at them, its girth larger than expected, its tongue flicking. First Son reaches for a stone to throw at what he thinks is the old crocodile, wanting to show off for his friends, but a sudden feeling in his gut freezes him and sends him hastily retreating down the path, followed by the other children. Looking over his shoulder he sees the head continuing to rise higher above the waters, visible now on top of a long, erect, sinewy neck, its back lined with pointed crests. The creature crawls from the water on muscular legs atop a massive, snake-like body, violently shaking the water off. This is not a crocodile. It is the Dragon found in their tribe's campfire stories, the one their parents frighten them with when they misbehave. It is real, and it is coming for them. As the children, breathless, approach the hoped for safety of their village, they are relieved to hear the frustrated roars of the Dragon receding into the distance. Traces of burnt sulfur and vegetation linger in the air. First Son sees his mother, the tribe's Spirit Walker, angrily waiting for him with crossed arms. She doesn't look happy.

ΔΔΔΔ

13. Destiny Revealed
"Encountering"

The First Son

Her son is right. She is not happy. That was the last thought Spirit Walker heard from her son's mind before her consciousness snapped back. Looking down the trail, she watches her son appear, trailed by a flock of panting children. He stops before her, shrugs, and starts to speak. "Don't bother. I don't need any more of your stories," she said. "I know exactly what happened out there today." A puzzled look comes over First Son's face. "Let me put it to you as simply as I can, First Son. If you weren't my eldest son and hadn't just had a birthday, today you and the other children would be dead. And not just you -- maybe even the whole village as well. I can't say it any plainer." First Son looks confused and a little scared. "A dragon, really? The Spirit Father? Are you crazy? Remember the impulse that hit you when you picked up that rock, stopping you dead in your tracks? That was my doing. If I hadn't grabbed hold of you, you'd all be dragon chow by now. Spirit Father must be approached with respect and proper ritual. But that's not all. There is something else you need to know. Our family has certain capabilities that begin to appear when we hit eighteen years of age, as you did on the last full moon. Your nascent psychic capabilities are just now beginning to emerge. That means I can look inside your mind. I shared the experiences of your little misadventure by the swamp. Know that you have a destiny now. Time to grow up. Buckle down and learn to use your powers to serve your tribe."

Δ

14. In the Well of Souls
"Inner Truth"

The Rider

The Rider is suspended within the walls of a giant, cylindrically shaped chamber. He is surrounded on all sides by striated, sandy colored cliffs, whose scope is so enormous that he is only able to see a small segment of them at a time. Twisting his long neck to look around him, he cannot see the top or bottom edges of the cavern. His long body is suspended on giant reptilian wings, held aloft by a gentle but persistent warm updraft. He flies once more as the Dragon. While floating there, he has no thoughts, no sense of identity, and no memories of having been there before. As more of the scene comes into focus, he realizes the cliff walls are not solid but are punctuated by a scattered series of small dark recessions. His field of view suddenly zooms in on an area to his right containing several of these recessed features. He sees now these are actually small caves set into the sides of the cliffs, big enough to contain only a single individual. Some caves are close together and others isolated and far apart. As he gets closer still he sees the caves are not empty. Each cave contains a solitary individual sitting cross-legged in its mouth. The individuals are both men and women, dressed in a wide variety of different garments, some primitive and others more contemporary.

∆∆∆

15. Choosing the Mystic Path
"Humbleness"

The Seeker

The Seeker, sitting in a trance, sees images of two adjacent caves. The caves are set into the sides of a cliff. Each cave occupies half his visual field. A fuzzy, amorphous border separates them, as if he were looking through binoculars, with each cave appearing in a distinct eyepiece. At the front of each cave he sees a similar sight: a man sitting in a relaxed cross-legged lotus position, eyes closed, lost in meditation. Each is a grizzled looking, 50ish years old, Eastern European man. Both are dressed similarly, in dark clothes wearing a loose over coat and a "peasant" cap. The only real difference in the apparel of the two is that the man on the left wears brown clothes and the man on the right blue grey clothes. Their appearance is so similar that they might be brothers or even fraternal twins. He has the distinct impression that in spite of the obvious similarities, these are two distinct individuals from different time frames who both happen to be mystics. He also considers that each of these men might be himself in a previous incarnation, or perhaps distant relatives from his own past. He realizes he has a choice to make. He would have to enter the cave at either the left or at the right. Without making any conscious choice, he is soon drawn into the cave on the left. He quickly zooms past the immobile figure into dark tunnels leading deeper into the cliffs.

∆∆

The "Hidden Source" Narrative:

Choosing to descend deeper into
the Under World, the Traveller is taken
by the Teacher to witness
the secret ritual of Soul energy cultivation,
before moving into the deepest core of consciousness,
traveling down the hidden river in the Cavern of Gems on the
way to a return to the surface, where he survives
the pull of the White Light,
leading to a new door:
the Tree of Worlds

ELEMENTAL DOMAIN:
EARTH

Descending into Hidden Fields

16. The Three Sisters
"Unity"

The Witness

Floating in an empty void, the Witness hears several voices talking, apparently somewhere above him. He cannot make out what they are saying. Looking up, he sees three separate, rectangular shaped windowed areas, floating in empty space, lined up next to each other. The boundaries between them are not sharp, but appear fuzzy and amorphous. In each window the head of a different woman is visible, all having straight brown hair and facial features and all roughly the same age, being in their mid thirties. All of these women are speaking, sometimes while facing each other, sometimes not, sometimes taking turns, sometimes talking all at once. Are they talking to each other? He is unsure. Try as he might, he cannot make out what they are saying. Initially believing that this was some kind of strange psychic chat room, he soon realizes after further observation they are not speaking to one another but instead to some unseen party in each of their own windows. The Traveller has one more revelation. He realizes that not only do these three women look enough alike to be sisters, but they also each resemble the Teacher figure he has seen before. Could there be more than one Teacher?

ΔΔΔ

17. The Fire Ritual
"The Family"

The Teacher

The Teacher stands before the Traveller in a dimly lit rock tunnel. She leads him through it into a large cave. Water trickles down its sides, forming a viscous black pool towards the back. In the center of the cave a large bonfire is burning. Concentric circles of primitively dressed women sit around it. They are loudly drumming and chanting in a language he does not recognize. Suddenly everything stops. As if on cue, everyone shouts and jumps to their feet, waving their hands over their heads with arms outstretched. A figure materializes next to the fire's surging flames, the Vision Dancer. She has dark features and black hair and for clothing wears only strips of leather across her top and bottom. As the crowd chants and stomps and drums, the mysterious figure starts to spin in wild gyrations, flinging her body around the fire in ecstatic frenzy. The faster she moves and spins, the higher the flames surge. Some movement inside the white smoke rising from the fire grabs his attention. He sees a 3-D image forming inside it, which as he watches soon resolves into a vivid, real time, and holographic-like image of the scene occurring before him. The Teacher catches his eye, and smiling at him, looks up at the smoke and claps her hands. The smoke suddenly disappears, along with everyone in the cavern. Nothing remains except for the fire and the black pool. Even the Teacher is gone.

∆∆∆∆

18. Through the Empty Worlds
"Alienation"

The Witness

The Witness hovers above a dark pool at the back of the cave. Muted greyed light flickers across its surface, reflecting light from a still burning fire. Suddenly he's pulled towards the pool and into its viscous depths. While moving through the pool, he initially loses all sense of time and soon after that all sense of motion. He is lost in its empty black void. His sense of self momentarily disappears as well. He soon finds himself not only moving again, but also once more possessed of spatial awareness. He floats within the center of a giant spherical chamber, as if he were a pinpoint of awareness within the hollow expanse of his own skull. He now feels himself moving further outwards and upwards. He crosses what appears to be an enclosing wall, as the texture of the region changes abruptly. A section of the wall dissolves before him. Hovering above the wall, he examines this open section and its well-defined architecture and structure. The wall itself is part of a curved shell enclosing an enormous black expanse. The wall texture is sponge-like in nature. It has repeating patterns of thin walled hexagons, like a honeycombed beehive. Nothing is visible inside these hexagons, with the bulk of the wall's mass empty space. The color of their edges, as well as their insides, is black. When the light of his awareness passes over them, the edges light up with a dull grey.

ΔΔ

19. Gorge of the Crystal River
"Containment"

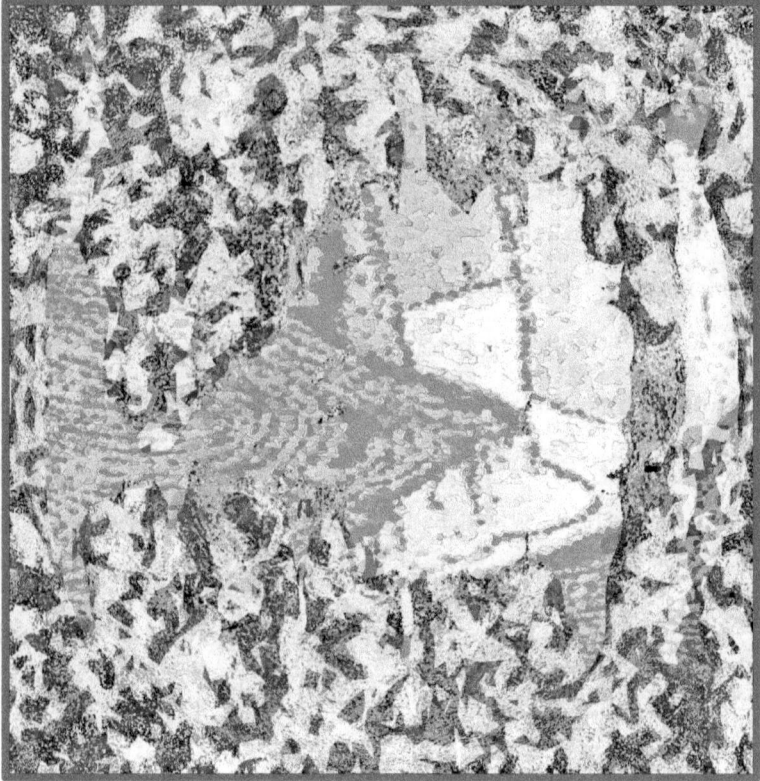

The Witness

The Witness is deep underground, with jagged stonewalls pressing on him. His awareness is initially fixed, focused on an area immediately above him, towards his right. He soon is moving forward, propelled at a steady pace through a twisting, cavern-like tunnel that cuts through the mountain around him. Everything is dark except for a narrow sphere of golden illumination shining out from the center of his awareness. Passing close by, he sees craggy protuberances covered with regions of crystalline facets and reflective gold, bouncing the light in a multitude of directions, dazzling his awareness with a fireworks-like display of brightly lit, glistening golden hues. Looking down, he is following the meandering path of a deep crevasse winding its way through the mountain, carved out by the waters of a cascading, rapidly flowing river. The river, illuminated by the light of his awareness, is a surprisingly rich shade of blue, even though there is no sky above for it to reflect. Foamy areas of the river reflect the bright golden color of the light from above. The river is moving in the same direction as he is but at a greater velocity. He studies the different patterns of its flow that gyrate beneath him as he tunnels through the mountain's interiors.

ΔΔΔ

20. Escaping the Dark Rift
"Liberation"

The Witness

The Witness moves underground through a dark tunnel. He perceives alternating areas of dark shadows and dim light moving past him, all rendered in shades of grey. The light is coming from some unseen source ahead of him. Twisting and turning through gloomy channels, the oscillating patterns of light and dark come faster and faster, like on a speeding subway train. Suddenly, rounding a sharp corner, a small area of dim white light becomes visible in the distance. The light's shape is not round. The closer he gets, the more rough and jagged it appears. The tunnel's exit is now visible, ahead and above him, opening into a brightly lit region. He experiences a quick moment of discontinuity. He is in the jagged opening for only an instant, before shooting into the sky. He catches the briefest glimpses of the landscape rushing by in greens and browns. Soon he sees only a bright blue sky punctuated by fluffy white clouds. He looks for the sun, for that is his goal. After the darkness, he longs for the pure light. But the sun is behind the clouds. Soon he is immersed inside a misty fog-like area of diffuse greyish white light. All color and features have completely vanished. He must be in the clouds. He continues to move upwards, as the light grows brighter and brighter, trying to escape the clouds. The light remains rendered only in shades of hazy grey. He still hopes to see the clear unadulterated source of this light, but greys are all he finds.

ΔΔ

21. White Light Blocked
"Hindrance"

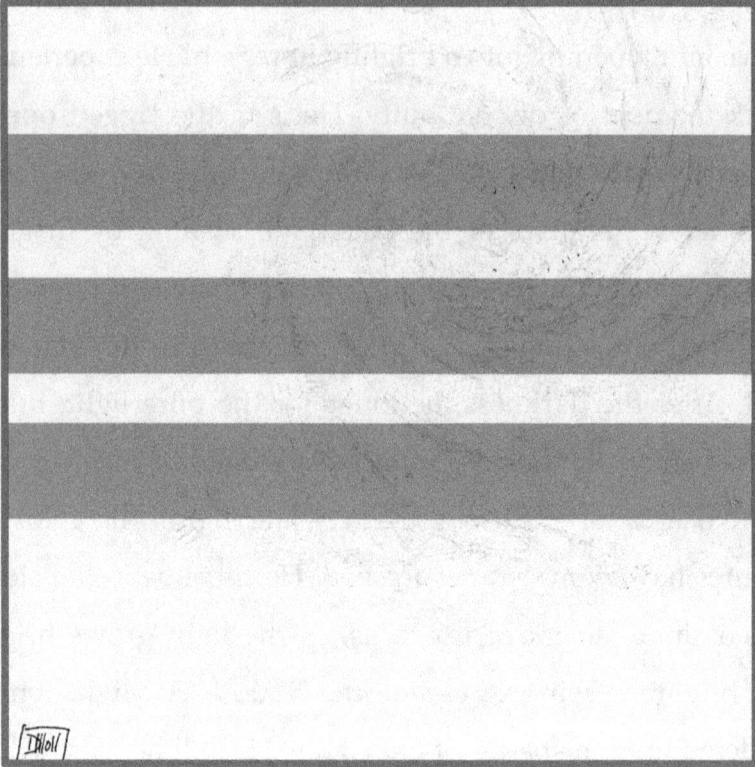

The Seeker

The Seeker, floating in trance, sees a solid white void. It lacks any texture or variation of light or shadow, more like a smooth sheet of blank paper than an open navigable expanse. Though hovering in place, the Seeker feels himself separated from this empty whiteness, as if it were a solid object for his perusal. At this point there is no impression of depth, only flatness. This sense of flatness disappears as the Seeker starts to slowly drift towards the upper right corner of the empty tableau. He is now inside the whiteness, being pulled into its depths. A vortex-like disturbance forms in the area to which he is being drawn. Small at first, the vibrating distortion begins to grow in size and intensity, as does the magnitude of the pulling force. A line from an old movie come to him, "Do not go into the light." This area is now like a white broiling sun, with light blinding in its intensity. He is being drawn closer and closer to this turbulent white fire, like a fish being pulled out of its dark watery depths into blinding sunlight. Suddenly, like a gate slamming shut, three black horizontal bars materialize across the center of his visual field, obscuring the boiling vortex. Shadowy rays of light stream through the bars from the anomaly, but enough of its gravitational force has been disrupted to stop his forward progress. Once again he floats in place, bathed now in streams of soft white light.

ΔΔΔ

22. The Tree of Worlds
"Develop Gradually"

The Witness

The Witness is in a forest glen, before a grove of trees. A particular tree in the center of the scene catches his attention. Then, everything disappears except for this single tree, suspended in a field of diffuse mist. As he watches, the tree begins to change. Its features coalesce, losing their details. He now sees a flattened two-dimensional, skeletal rendering of a tree-shaped exemplar. All its leaves disappear. New spherical shaped leaves begin to appear, brown, semi-translucent tokens that dangle like ornaments from the tree's twisting branches. The tree continues to change, slowly growing in girth and in height. The leaves also grow in diameter, though faster than the tree. Where before the canopy of leaves was a pale brown, a rich bouquet of bright colors now blooms, spanning all colors of the rainbow. Continuing to grow in richness and brightness, the leaves glow with their own internal source of colored light. The shape of the leaves also becomes more three-dimensional. They have doubled in size and are shaped like square-edged glass lenses, serving as windows for peering into other worlds. Even though the leaves are glowing orbs of light, the body of the tree and its branches are still monochromic and flat, creating a stark contrast between the dark tree and its colorful crown of spectral fruit.

ΔΔΔ

The "Castle Redemption" Narrative:

Now perched on an Upper World high mountain plateau, as a
young Apprentice Blacksmith in a medieval kingdom,
the Traveller pursues his destiny, where, fleeing the Dragon
and drafted into the King's service,
he procures the Shadow Warrior's dark powers
for the King and receives the mysterious Golden Key,
before confronting a new door:
an elaborate clockworks puzzle mechanism

ELEMENTAL DOMAIN:
MOUNTAIN

Standing Firm before the Darkness

23. The Valley of Solitary Oaks
"Childhood"

The Witness

Rising up through dark waters, the Witness hovers above a blue river meandering through a verdant mountain valley, brightly lit by sunlight in a cloud sprinkled sky. Ranges of blue grey mountains fade into the distance. They surround a series of small rolling hills, each crowned with a single majestic oak tree and nothing else. The greens of the valley are saturated, glowing with the fresh growth of new spring. The Witness gets the impression that he is inside a pastoral landscape painting. The Witness view quickly moves from hill to hill and tree to tree, growing ever closer to the surrounding peaks, not knowing what is driving his movements. He stops at a hill where he sees the Teacher perched before the hill's tree. She approaches the tree and peels back the bark from its wide trunk, revealing a hidden, arched shaped area built in the tree. Some kind of apparatus is contained there. Manipulating an unseen mechanism, she folds down a chair connected to the tree. She sits on it, her back to the tree, facing a nearby mountain range. Suddenly the Witness' gaze is pulled away from the seated Teacher and rapidly propelled into the air, flying up the side of the highest visible mountain slope. He sees only blue sky and clouds rushing at him.

Δ

24. The Dragon Watch
"Small Accumulation"

The Apprentice Blacksmith

The Apprentice Blacksmith stands on the leveled edge of a mountain outlook on a wooden platform. He is buffeted by high winds, as he gazes below right into a river valley formed by cascading rows of mountains receding into the distance. This valley looks familiar to him, and he is trying to pick out familiar landmarks. He is not alone on this outcrop, for there are several others standing behind him, talking and joking with one another. Still staring down into the valley, he is jostled by someone behind him, who tells him to do his job and watch the sky. He reminds himself why he is there. He is not a sightseer, but part of a group of Watchers, whose job it is to scan the skies above for signs of danger. Of course, as always, he is bored and restless, since nothing ever happens. He sees in the distance a dark flying shape. Probably just another large bird, he thinks to himself, maybe an eagle, looking to prey on the village's small animals. The shape gets larger and larger the closer it gets. As its features become clearer he realizes with a start that it is not a bird. It has enormous angular wings and a long body and neck. It is the Sky Dragon, and it is in search of larger prey. The Watchers sound the alarm and rush back to warn the village.

ΔΔ

25. Retreat to the Castle
"Retreat"

The Apprentice Blacksmith

The Apprentice Blacksmith runs across the flat, rocky plateau perched high above the mountain ranges that surround it. No trees are visible, only low scrub growth and sparse. Behind him are other members of the Watch, having sounded the alarm and passed through the village to rouse the recalcitrant from their beds, since the day is still young. Looking to his right, he sees what looks like the entire population of the village running alongside him, both young and old, dressed in the peasant garb of everyday life. The villagers looked relaxed, smiling as they run, not at all alarmed, thinking perhaps that this is just another random, unscheduled drill. Some turn to look at him, laughing at the serious expression they see portrayed on his face. They are treating this event as a footrace, trying to be the first to reach the blocky, grey stonewalls of the castle sitting on the hill above them. The castle's gates are open, something that is unusual for this time of day. In the sky above, the mournful cry of an ancient beast sounds, announcing the immanent arrival of the Sky Dragon. Its shadow drifts across the plateau like some black specter, creating alarm and confusion in the ranks of the now fleeing masses. The Apprentice pushes himself to run even faster, focused only on his destination, no longer glancing about.

ΔΔΔ

26. Called to the King's Service
"Small Crossing"

The Apprentice Blacksmith

The Apprentice Blacksmith enters the castle, immersed in the crowd of people fleeing the village, pushing and shoving in a frantic attempt to enter before the gates are closed. A short time later the Apprentice finds himself in a small chamber. Puzzled about where he is, he runs his hand over the rough square blocks of granite making up the wall before him, only inches from his face. Looking around, the Apprentice realizes he is alone in the darkened room. He has no idea about why he is here. As more of his senses return to him, he feels a weight pressing down on his back and shoulders. He discovers that he is wearing a shirt of grey rusty chainmail over his everyday clothes. Looking down at his chest, he sees that a soiled white tunic covers the chainmail, cinched with a rope for a belt. It has a large blue square in its center, with a strange looking coat-of-arms he does not recognize engraved on it. Its bottom half is shaped like an upturned horseshoe, with each end topped by an oval shape. A shaft runs up its center with a diamond shape at its top. Turning behind him, he realizes a door has opened, casting light into the small alcove in which he stands, revealing a view of a rocky plain outside the walls.

ΔΔΔ

27. The Shadow Warrior

"Contention"

The Apprentice Blacksmith

Sent alone from the castle to face the Dark Army's champion, the Apprentice Blacksmith carries no weapon. For armor he wears only ill-fitting rusted chainmail and a torn, soiled tunic, secured with a rope for a belt. There the Shadow Warrior waits, massive, standing over 7 feet tall, his impassive face broad and features coarse. He is fitted with black leather armor and leggings, covered with silver spikes and studs. Even at a distance he towers over him. The Apprentice hesitantly walks towards the Shadow Warrior. Suddenly the Warrior lunges at him, swinging wildly, as the Apprentice frantically slips and dodges beneath his blows. He takes heart in seeing that the Shadow Warrior's movements are stiff and awkward. The Shadow Warrior is too big for him to hurt with strikes. Remembering his training, the Apprentice deflects a wild left, and using its momentum to pull it across his body, sweeps the Warrior's leading leg out from under him. The Shadow Warrior goes down hard, striking his head on the rocky ground, losing consciousness. Black swirling vapors begin to flow from the Shadow Warrior's mouth and nose. Quickly the Apprentice crouches over him to harvest the escaping Shadow Energies, rapidly inhaling them before they could dissipate. He must get these to the King.

ΔΔ

28. Empowering the King
"Replenishing"

The Apprentice Blacksmith

The Apprentice Blacksmith is standing on the barren fields outside the castle walls. He burns with the Shadow Energy swirling inside him that he captured from the Shadow Warrior. He turns and sees the King approaching him, alone and without the retinue of guards that normally accompany him. More surprisingly, the King stops and kneels on one knee, beckoning him to come close. He approaches the King with hesitant steps, and stopping before him, bows his head in a sign of supplication. He knows what the King expects him to do. The King looks up at him as he exhales the black vapors of the Shadow Energy directly into the King's open mouth. The King seems to grow in stature and vitality as he absorbs the freed vapors. The next thing he knows, he and the King are standing on a rocky plain with the assembled forces of the Dark Army spread out before them. None of the King's army is present, only the two of them. The King tells him he is there only as witness. What he witnesses is remarkable. Standing aside, he observes the ensuing battle, as the King sweeps through the attacking multitudes as if they were made of paper, rendering them literally into clouds of dust with swirling swords held in each of his hands.

ΔΔΔ

29. Grant of the Golden Key
"Increasing"

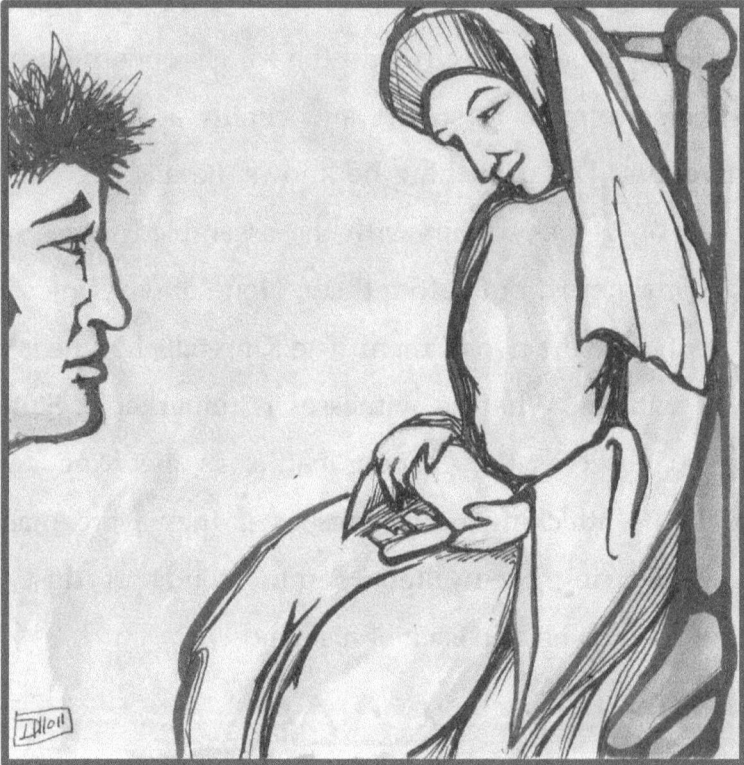

The Apprentice Blacksmith

The Apprentice Blacksmith is within the depths of the castle. He stands in a candle lit, furnished room on one of the castle's lower, heavily guarded floors. He doesn't know why he is here. In walks a woman of regal bearing, wearing a long ornate white and lavender dress with a flowing headpiece. Looking closely at her face, he recognizes her as the Teacher.

She directs him to sit in a plain, squarish wooden chair, while she sits in an elaborately carved, high-backed, throne-like chair, facing him. He sees that in her lap she is cradling an object wrapped in plush, violet colored, velvet cloth. She looks down at this object and then at him and smiles. She peels back the cloth to show him what she is holding. It is an elaborately crafted skeleton key, about eight inches in length, made of solid gold that sparkles in the candle light. She bows her head to him ever so subtly and hands him the key, which he receives in his two trembling, outstretched hands. He is surprised by its weight. He has no idea about whether the key is merely ceremonial or the solution to some locked door waiting for him in his future. He straps the key to his back.

$$\Delta\Delta\Delta\Delta$$

30. The Clockworks Enigma
"Not Yet Across"

The Apprentice Blacksmith

Leaving the castle, with the Golden Key in hand, the Apprentice Blacksmith walks down a long, dark, narrow corridor, lit by sporadically located torches. As he winds his way through the seemingly endless labyrinth, he spies a light ahead and increases his pace towards the hoped for exit. Getting closer, he sees that it is way out of the tunnels, but also that a metal gate blocks the opening. The gate, which covers the whole exit, is made of elaborately shaped cast iron. The gate contains three rows of three rectangular-shaped metal compartments, with all the rectangles except the central one containing different designs of spiral shapes imbedded in a circular frame. The central square is solid, with an eight-sided emblem embossed on its surface. He notices that this central area does not contain a keyhole where he could use the golden key he carries strapped to his back. As he examines the gate with his hands, he discovers that the circular components can be rotated and that they are connected to elements of a clockworks mechanism that lies beneath them. By rotating the circular component in either a clockwise or counterclockwise direction a specified amount, he learns that the piece can be removed and potentially swapped with one of the other pieces. He realizes that in order to open the gate, he must remove the circular pieces and reassemble them in the correct order. He examines the emblem on the central piece more closely, searching for clues to help him get started.

Δ

ᚷhe "Pyramid Ascension" Narrative:

Continuing his ascension as the Adept, a cloned member of a
secret society in an ancient high desert realm, the Traveller
survives rituals of selection to ascend to the rank of
Journeyman, gaining entry into the sacred Pyramid and the
White Tower, ultimately leading to a meeting with the
Teacher and the Magister at the Council of Elders,
before passing through a new door:
the Blue Door

ELEMENTAL DOMAIN:
HEAVEN

Ascending into Power

31. The Prism of Rainbow

"Truth"

The Seeker

Sitting in meditative trance, the Seeker sees a blank white region spread out before him. In its center a translucent, triangular shaped object begins to form, with three sides of equal length. As he is pulled closer and closer to this object, he recognizes that it is a glass prism, with two flat extruded sides and a base. Now he is inside the object. Looking diagonally up and out the left and right sides, he sees nothing outside the prism but empty white space. Within the prism a diffuse sphere of golden light begins to form around him. As the sphere of light grows brighter, it starts to coalesce, become more opaque. Rays flow out from it, illuminating more of the prism's interior. Once the inside of the prism is totally engulfed in this golden light, the prism itself begins to transform. Its sides grow and fold around each other, until what remains is a four-sided translucent pyramid enclosing the pulsing golden light. This light now spreads out through the pyramid's four walls. The Seeker sees that for each side, spectrums of multicolored spheres of light are projected upwards and outwards, bathing the once empty space in shimmering rays of incandescent colors.

∆∆∆∆

32. The Village of Adepts
"Multitude"

The Witness

Next to a wide, languidly flowing river, the Witness, looking down to his right, sees a primitive village, mud huts with straw roofs scattered across open fields. In the distance he spies the desert dunes and the top of what appears to be a pyramid. Palm trees and lush vegetation line the riverbanks, but there is nothing growing amid the huts, the yellow sandy ground worn bare and hard packed by constant traffic. Initially the village appears empty, but then, as if from a signal, individuals start pouring from the huts. From his viewpoint hovering above them, they all look similar in appearance, with brown skin and short black hair, identical in size and build. They appear Middle Eastern in nationality. All appear young, maybe in their mid 20's, with no older individuals in sight. He sees no one supervising or giving them any kind of direction. They are all uniformly dressed, with loose white pants and short-sleeved white tunics. They are all barefoot. Their movements appear un-choreographed, though they are all engaged in the same activity, spinning and swinging long wooden staffs, as they randomly wander among their camp, somehow avoiding each other. From what he observes, the scene looks to the Witness like some kind of impromptu martial arts training facility, with its own kind of strange balletic grace.

Δ

33. Advancement to Candidacy
"Perseverance"

The Adept

The Adept, dressed in short-sleeved white tunic and baggy pants, stands on a dirt-covered field, staring at the pyramid in the distance. Surrounding him on all sides are dozens of his peers, all identically dressed. All have dark brown skin and short black hair and are androgynous in appearance. But these individuals do not just look alike. He notices that their appearance is identical in all respects, as would be the case if they were identical twins or clones. In the distance he sees several much taller individuals dressed similarly to him and carrying short staffs. They're involved in some kind of selection process, in which they walk up to certain Adepts and tap them on the shoulder with the staff. When they do this, the Adept would immediately collapse to the ground. He asks one of the nearby Adepts what is happening. Are these fallen Adepts dead or hurt? The other Adept replies that today is "Selection Day." He is not sure if that is a good thing or a bad thing. Is he worthy of advancement? Soon, he sees one of the Selectors heading directly for him. As the Selector comes up to him, the Selector nods, and then taps him on the shoulder. He feels himself crumbling to the ground, but even as his consciousness slips away, he feels no fear.

ΔΔ

34. Gathering of the Dragon Clan
"Great Strength"

The Adept

The Adept, waking from his trance, finds himself walking on a broad boulevard lined with towering palm trees. The boulevard is a scene of bustling activity, with many merchants selling their wares on the side of the road. He sees a great pyramid rising up like a mountain at the end of the roadway. It size is so massive that its pinnacle is lost in the low hanging clouds of a brewing storm. He is accompanied by a small group of his fellow Adepts, all identical in dress and appearance to him, with brown skin and short black hair, dressed all in white. They are all bunched tightly together, seemingly unsure of themselves. He is feeling strange and disoriented; his whole body is vibrating, especially his head, which felt like it contained a hive of bees. He feels like he is changing. Recovering more of his senses, he remembers that he has survived the selection process. But he has no idea what comes next. Ahead of them waits a gathering of tall, heavily muscled individuals. They are not wearing the customary white tunics of their order, but are instead dressed in warrior garb, with shining gold armor. They all carry large spears and wear from what his vantage point looks like ornate green headpieces on their heads. As he gets closer he realizes that these are not helmets, for he can now see now their true face. They stand upright, but they are not entirely human. Their heads are the heads of dragons. From his training, he knows them as the Dragon Clan.

ΔΔ

35. The Golden Corridor
"Treading"

The Journeyman

The Journeyman walks through the narrow, dark, tunnels of the ancient pyramid. The corridors are hewn out of rough rock, squarish in shape. Other similarly attired individuals accompany him. All, like him, are wearing khaki pants and vests over loosely fitting white shirts. He alone wears a broad rimmed safari hat. The tunnel narrows further until rounding a corner it suddenly becomes wider. Its formerly downward slope now begins to curve upwards. The walls, no longer square, become much more rounded. The walls and floors are now smooth and metallic, more like the rounded corridors of a vessel than a passage through a rocky mound. The corridor curves upwards sharply to the left. Looking at the inside wall, a golden sphere of light follows his gaze. The wall, crafted out of solid gold, is not bare, but covered with row after row of engraved hieroglyphs and symbols, a strange blend of Egyptian, Hebrew, Chinese and Greek markings. A bright white glow emanates from the unseen area around the corner. The curved gold walls abruptly end, replaced by a chamber with white walls. He hears machinelike sounds of humming.

ΔΔ

36. Climbing the White Tower
"The Wanderer"

The Journeyman

The Journeyman is on the ground floor of a towering structure. Looking about, he does not see any exit or doors. He does not know where he is. The walls of the structure, which appear metallic in composition, are curved, giving it a cylindrical shape. Gazing up, he sees that the tower's central area is open. There are no solid floors spanning the tower beyond the one on which he stands. Everything within the tower is colored a stark white, except for the silver colored railing that runs along the outer side of the walkways. He sees no furnishings or objects of any kind that break up the monotony of the tower's sterile environment or provide any clues about its purpose. He begins to climb the walkways that spiral up the inside walls of the tower, always looking for some sign of other people, as well as a way to get out. But he sees no evidence of other people or any doors or windows. Periodically, he comes across balcony platforms that are suspended out from the walkways, accessible by stairs. He dutifully climbs each one he encounters, looking for clues to the reason for his presence in this tower. But there is nothing to see. He climbs and he climbs. As he nears the top, he discovers that there is a glass-enclosed structure suspended from the roof. He quickens his pace and heads for it.

Δ

37. The Council of Elders
"Turning Back"

The Traveller

The Traveller enters a glass chamber suspended on beams within a circular white tower. Turning around, he discovers the Teacher. She directs his attention to the walls of the chamber. He now stands in a square white room containing only a single Blue Door. The Teacher opens the door and leads him down a long white corridor with doors on both sides. She stops and opens a door on the left, indicating that he should go inside. The room contains a large rectangular table stretching back to the far wall. The walls are covered floor to ceiling with overflowing bookshelves. Seated around the table are nine white bearded, distinguished looking gentlemen, four on each side and one at the far end, the Magister. He notices an empty chair at the end of the table near him. Standing up, the Magister welcomes him to the Council of Elders and gestures for him to sit. The Traveller looks down and recognizes a much younger version of himself. He feels too young and inexperienced to be in their presence. Turning to leave, he says, "I don't belong here. I'm only a Neophyte." Walking away, the Teacher by his side, he hears the Magister say, "You are much more than that, Traveller. No matter where you go or who you are, your journey will always bring you back here."

ΔΔ

The "Spirit Incursion" Narrative

The Seeker, having achieved a certain level of ascension in his
visionary travels and passed through the Eight Doors, now
experiences the descent of spiritual power prophesized
in the Nexus Formation narrative, becoming energetically
transformed and witness to a series of visions in the mundane
world, symbolic of different states of energy
depicted on the Post-Heaven Bagua diagram

POST-HEAVEN BAGUA

Yin rotation

Awakening within the Mundane World

38. Lights in the Darkness
"Influence"

The Seeker

The Seeker sits in his room, meditating. He is still present in the mundane world, feeling his body and aware of his surroundings. Following his practice, he stares at the shifting dark shapes drifting behind his closed eyes. As his breathing slows, he slips deeper into the first stages of the meditational trance. Suddenly there is a bright flash of orange-yellow light.

It briefly illuminates his entire visual field before quickly fading out. It disappears as quickly as it had appeared. As if the first pulse was a test firing, the flash returns again, and this time persists, blinking quickly on and off with a constant frequency, each pulse lasting about a second. This continues for about thirty seconds. The flashing occurs at a pace driven by its own internal rhythm. It is not coordinated with either his heart rate or breathing cycles, as might have been expected. What drives this phenomenon remains a mystery, even as it continues to sporadically appear as an element in subsequent meditation sessions.

$$\Delta\Delta\Delta$$

39. The Descent of Power
"Receptivity"

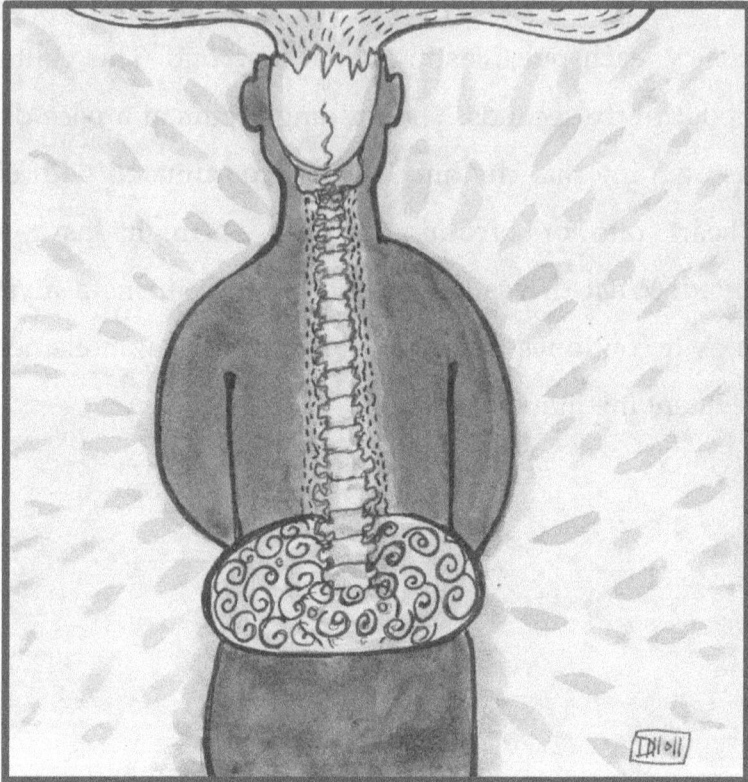

The Seeker

From deep trance the Seeker lurches awake to discover his heart racing and breath panting. His eyes spring open. He is in his room, sitting in his meditation chair, as expected. But all is not normal. The room itself is shaking. Quiet ambient meditation music had been playing on a portable CD player set on the floor in the corner of the room to his left. It is quiet no more. The CD is now emphatically stuck in a repeating loop, rapidly skipping back and forth, like a defective vinyl record. The sound is so loud and cacophonous that the Seeker is unable to form any thoughts about what is happening. The crown of the Seeker's head feels as if it has been pried open, with flowing, electric energy rushing down his spine. A completely new, unexpected sensation, it continues to overload his capacity for reflective thought. This fiery energy spirals unabated down his back, penetrating to the base of his spine, where it collects in an expanding pool of vibrating, liquid heat. The flow keeps coming and coming until the Seeker can take no more, his ability to absorb any additional energy lost, his reservoir full. He feels like he is vibrating all over, as the accumulated power pushes to escape its bodily confinement. Shaking, he feels trapped in its grace and power, his Self lost in the depths of its ecstasy.

Δ

40. Flight of the Firebird
"Fire"

The Seeker

The Seeker has ended the meditation session in which the Descent had occurred. Back in the mundane world, he has left his meditation room and gone downstairs, where he is standing next to the side window by the dining room table. He is still somewhat shaken by the events of his session. He looks over the deck past the nearby trees towards the adjacent pond, as he tries to understand the nature of what he had just experienced. Suddenly something catches his eye as a bird zips by the window over the deck. Now on alert, he notices more detail about the bird as it quickly returns, flying in a tight loop near the window. The bird is medium sized and a brilliant, solid scarlet red in color. Its wings are sharply angled and its head pointed, making it look almost like a miniature fighter jet. The bird continues to fly tight aerobatic turns and spins and loops in front of the window for about thirty seconds before disappearing, never to be seen again. He has the distinct impression that this performance was specifically intended for him.

$$\Delta\Delta\Delta$$

41. The Spirit Wings Unfold
"Wind"

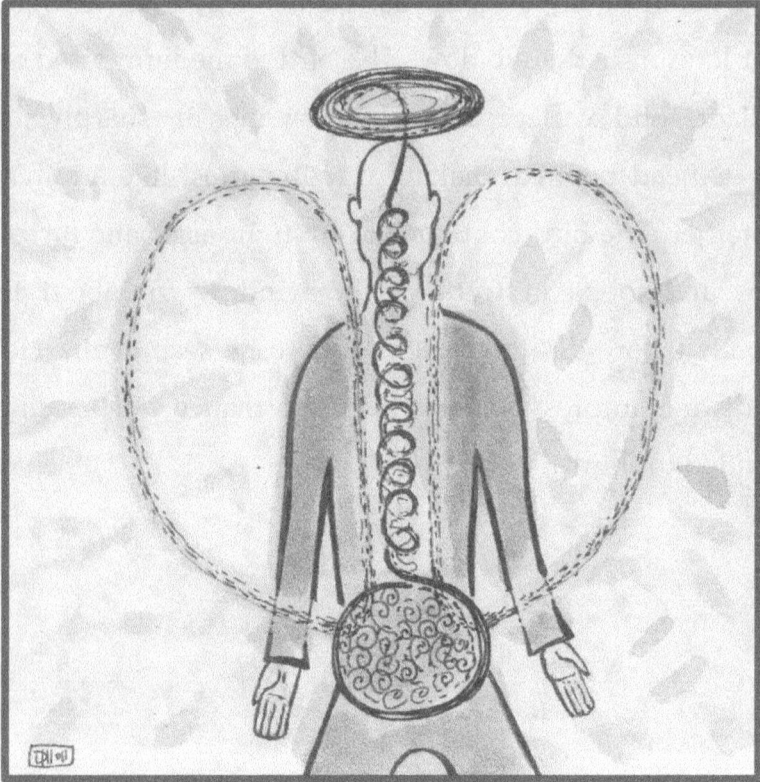

The Seeker

The Seeker is sitting in his room, meditating. As he starts to slip into a deeper trance, a loud, high pitched shriek abruptly snaps him back into his physical body. The sound reminded him of the shrill cry of a bird of prey. At the same time, he feels his spine being ripped into three pieces down its vertical axis, one piece pulled to the right and the other to the left.

Maybe the sound he heard was this rip. Where before there had been one channel, he now feels three, the original central channel of the spinal column and two new auxiliary channels, one on each side. He feels warm, vibrant energy spiraling up the central channel from a seemingly endless reservoir in his lower torso, where exiting the crown of his head, it begins to circulate in the shape of a halo above his head. At the same time, subtle energy flows stream directly up the two side channels and exit next to each shoulder. Each column curves up and out past his ears before flowing back down in a oval shaped stream to the base of the spine to re-enter its original side channel. The two distinct energy flows trace out the shape of wings on each side of his body. He feels like he has emerged from a cocoon and been reborn with a new Etheric body.

ΔΔ

42. Explosion's Echo
"Thunder"

The Seeker

The Seeker is sitting in his room meditating, deep in trance, lost in a state of deep, empty absence. Within this empty state, something calls to him, igniting a spark that gives rise to a tiny kernel of consciousness. As more of his senses return to him, he hears, seemingly in the distance, a deep rumbling roar. Then, suddenly snapping back to full consciousness in the mundane world, he is rocked by thunderous waves of explosive sound. The room itself seems to shake, and he would be tempted to believe that lightening had struck nearby, except that he sees that it is a perfectly clear, sunlit morning outside. After about 5 more seconds of violent sound, the explosive echoes fade away, to be replaced by the normal sounds of the morning. No events within his immediate environment can account for what roused him so precipitously from his meditation.

ΔΔΔΔ

43. In the Arms of the Titan
"Keeping Still"

The Seeker

The Seeker is sitting in his room, meditating. Sinking deeper into trance, he is still aware of himself and his situation. He suddenly feels that he is not alone in his room, as he senses a nearby presence. The sensation of another presence grows even stronger until he feels that this entity is right in front of him. He feels a large mass looming over him. He sits very still, unsure about what is happening around him, but not wanting to reveal his awareness of its presence. Though his eyes are closed, he sees an image superimposed upon the dark field visible behind his closed eyelids. It is the translucent, shimmering shape of a large, hulking humanoid form, with spread arms moving to encircle him. At the same time he feels, as an energetic force against his body, the presence of two large hands on his upper back. Their presence seems benevolent to him, as if he is being sheltered and protected by the entity leaning over him, though from what he does not know. Although he is unable to make out any of the distinguishing features of this entity, since he experiences it only as an energetic pressure and afterimage behind his closed eyes, he somehow knows who it is. It is the Shadow Warrior, returned from an earlier vision of the Apprentice Blacksmith.

Δ

44. Lost in the Dark Abyss
"Darkness"

The Seeker

The Seeker is sitting in meditation lost in deep trance, unaware of himself or his surroundings. As if a switch has been flicked, his consciousness suddenly blossoms into being, but only as a primitive awareness of raw presence. This presence brings no sense of self or identity, no thoughts or feelings, no physical sensations. These aspects manifest themselves entirely as a sense of absence, leaving only the barest form of a being-here-now. The "here" is as much of a mystery to his awareness as the mystery of his identity is. The pervading mystery is all there is, a mystery which manifests itself in sensation in the form of a deep, black, empty void – a blackness deeper than black. After an indeterminate amount of time passes in this dark emptiness, a small flame springs into life. It takes the form of a single thought: "Where am I?" Whatever the source of this thought, it serves as the seed for the genesis of a more expansive awareness. He remembers where he is and soon thereafter who he is. His sense of physical form likewise begins to return, but strangely not as a body sitting in his meditation chair. Rather, he feels as if his body is hovering in space to the left of the chair.

ΔΔΔ

45. When the Dragon Strikes
"Creation"

The Seeker

In quiet and deep trance the Seeker sits, lost in the void. Nothing stirring, nothing felt. Everything peaceful. No sensations penetrate this veil of silence. But then something stirs, awakening some of his senses. From the left something unseen and unthought appears, sensed only at first as a slight rustling beyond the periphery of his closed eyes. With his

Vision-Eyes now open, the Seeker turns his gaze leftwards to investigate the source of this interruption. He sees hovering next to the chair in which he sits a broad, green reptilian head. It has a long snout and protruding eyes, and it is looking right at him. The beast's head continues to rise and draw closer, suspended upon a long neck coiled above him, seemingly emerging out of empty space, a door opened into another dimension. The rest of the room seems entirely normal, as does the perceived mass of his body. He realizes that what he is seeing, somehow overlaid on the real world, is the head of a Dragon, mouth open, long pointed teeth flashing, tongue lolling, eyes glaring red with fiery intent. Suddenly, with neck uncoiling like a whip, the Dragon strikes, lunging at him with jaws snapping. The Seeker jerks from his semi-trance with a start, fueled by now present adrenalin. Still sitting in his chair, his body jerks to the right to avoid the Dragon's strike, even as the image of the Dragon dissolves like so much smoke into nothingness.

ΔΔ

46. Play of the White Tiger
"Joyful"

The Seeker

The Seeker is walking out in the mundane world, crossing the small bridge that spans the stream behind his house, accompanied by his wife. He begins to climb the three sections of steps that lead up a small hill to a grassy area that overlooks the pond far below. The steps are old railroad ties set into the side of a dirt-covered path. The ascending steps are in a zigzag configuration, with the first and third legs heading straight up the hill and the second leg cutting sharply across the hill at almost a 90-degree angle to the other two. The Seeker, turning to his left, starts up the second leg. At the end of this leg there is a banked area on the side of the hill with a small, flattened area at its top. Looking up the steps he's about to climb, he sees a quick flash of movement in this area. He believes a white animal head has just popped up and down. As he watches, it does this a couple more times. He recognizes it as the head of a cat, one much larger than a housecat. He asks his wife if she had seen the animal. The cat's head peers at him one more time; its white paws are perched to the side to prop it up. He quickly climbs to the top of the steps to examine the area where he saw the cat. He sees no signs of it and realizes that the topography of the area made what he had just seen impossible.

ΔΔΔΔ

The "Soul Revelation" Narrative

The Traveller, as the Seeker in the Under World, experiences a
ritual shamanic death at the hands of the Wolf, then to
confront a series of different personas, some from previous
visions and others from deep in his Soul,
before a final transfiguration liberates his Soul,
now revealed as the Teacher,
from its domain in his unconscious.

NARRATIVE DOMAIN:
WATER

Illusions Swept Away

47. The Hour of the Wolf
"Eradicating"

The Seeker

The Seeker, in trance, sees a younger version of himself, laying flat on the ground, back pressed against a sparsely grassed field, arms by his sides, palms up. This Other-Self is alive but not moving, his eyes closed. His demeanor appears contemplative, yoga-like, as if he awaits the arrival of some kind of revelation. From the Seeker's point of view, the scene is seen in perspective, with the subject's feet pointed towards the lower left and his head towards the upper right. A large grey white Wolf saunters into view from the right side of the scene. She moves lazily, not showing any haste or excitement, languid in her movements. After circling the body a few times, always in a counter-clockwise direction, the Wolf stops below the body, her nose facing the Other-Self's head. As the Seeker watches, the Wolf begins to feed on the head of the Other-Self, apparently intent on devouring his face. The Other-Self, surprisingly, continues to remain still, showing no reaction to what's happening to him. Even though the Seeker's perspective is now fluctuating between that of the observing witness and the subject of the Wolf's attention, he feels no pain or fear. When occupying the body of the Other-Self, he lies there calmly with eyes closed. He floats within a reddish dark void, feeling only a vague, distant, shaking pressure on his head.

∆∆∆

48. Behind the Raven Mask
"Hardship"

The Seeker

The Seeker is sitting in meditation. Slipping deeper into trance, he is still aware of himself and his situation. He sees the form of a head beginning to form in front of him, floating in space. As the head comes into focus, he realizes that the face is not visible but instead concealed behind some type of a dark mask. The mask completely obscures the front of the head, so that no other features such as hair or skin color are visible. Even the ears are hidden. The mask is painted a deep black and looks to be made of wood, with only a slight curvature to fit over the face. It does not look comfortable, but ill fitting and stiff, something worn as part of an initiatory ritual or some other kind of ceremonial gathering where one's identity must be hidden. The only openings it has are two holes for the eyes. The Seeker realizes with a start that the eyes do not look normal, but appear to be colored solid black, with no whites visible. A pointed protuberance is present where the nose would be. The Seeker recognizes that it is a long black beak, and that he is looking at a mask of the Raven. He does not know whom or what the mask conceals or its purpose in doing so.

$$\Delta\Delta\Delta\Delta$$

49. The Demon Dismissal

"Poison"

The Seeker

The Seeker sits in his room, meditating. Sinking deeper into trance but still aware of himself and his environment, he sees a face coming into focus, floating before him, as if he is looking into a mirror. The face is that of a younger man, long and narrow with angular cheekbones, dark eyes and straight brown hair. He soon realizes that he is seeing an image of his own face when he was about 35 years old. Following this recognition, the features of the face begin to morph into something else. The overall shape of the face distorts into a twisted version of itself. The mouth develops a sneer. The eye sockets become hollowed out and blackened around the edges, as if the eye had been burned out from within. The hair becomes wild and protrudes in snake-like clumps. A demon-like visage is now glaring back at him. In spite of its horrific appearance, he feels no emotion or apprehension, only a strange calmness. But his instincts tell him some response is required. He flexes some previously undiscovered internal muscles and with the gesture of an imaginary hand, sweeps the image of the demon away. He feels some satisfaction from this.

Δ

50. The Return of the King
"Exhausting"

The Seeker

The Seeker is sitting in his room, meditating. Sinking deeper into trance, but still aware of himself and his situation, he sees the shape of a head beginning to form in front of him, hovering in space. The head is male, with a long, narrow face and straight nose, framed by long, curly black hair down to his shoulders and a short beard with tight curls. Something about his appearance suggests to the Seeker that the individual is Greek. The Greek looks back at the Seeker with recognition in his eyes. His expression indicates that he has encountered the Seeker before. The Seeker stares back at the Greek, trying to identify where he might have seen him before. He remembers that he has seen the Greek not in the mundane world but in a vision, as the King served by the Apprentice Blacksmith. The Greek, noting a glimmer of recognition in the Seeker's eyes, winks at him and begins to speak: "I am the King of Chaos and have been active throughout history." For some reason, the name "Agamemnon" pops into the Seeker's mind. The Seeker wonders whether this being is the spreader of chaos or the source of order in a world beset by chaos.

ΔΔΔ

51. Shadow Communion
"Breaking Through"

The Seeker

The Seeker is sitting in his room, meditating. Sinking deeper into trance, but still aware of himself and his situation, he sees a face and torso coming into focus, suspended in the shimmering space before him. He recognizes the face as that of the Shadow Warrior, who he had previously confronted and bested in an earlier vision, leaving the Warrior immobilized on the ground. As before, the Warrior is dressed in black leather armor, covered with silver studs and short spikes. His features are broad and coarse, his eyes dark, his black beard and hair full and tangled. The Seeker examines the Warrior's features carefully, looking for some kind of clue about why he is seeing him again. The face remains impassive, though resolute in its gaze. The Warrior is looking straight ahead, as if to avoid eye contact with him. The Seeker realizes he feels no animosity while looking at the Warrior, viewing him more as a fellow traveler than a hostile force. This feels like a revelation to him, and, as if in recognition of this, the Warrior suddenly shifts his gaze and looks directly at him. As the Seeker watches, the Warrior's features begin to morph into someone else. He sees a younger version of his own face beginning to emerge.

ΔΔΔΔ

52. Necklace of the Spirit Walker
"Domesticated Maiden"

The Seeker

The Seeker is sitting in his room, meditating. Sinking deeper into trance, he is still aware of himself and his situation. He views a face coming into focus, suspended before him. He sees the face of a noble African woman, with smooth, chocolate-colored skin and very short black hair. She is staring straight ahead and is perfectly still. He recognizes this figure as the

Spirit Walker from the First Son visions. As more of the scene comes into view, he focuses on the woman's now visible shoulders and the top part of her torso. Her shoulders are bare, with the exception of a necklace draped across her shoulders, with vertical rows of beads hanging down that cover her chest. The beads are cylindrical in shape, stacked on top of each other. There are six beads on each string. The beads alternate in distinctive patterns of white and turquoise blue beads, with the same pattern present on all of the strings. The overall effect of these patterns is a series of six blue and white horizontal rows draped across her chest in a distinctive pattern, which from the top reads white blue, white blue, white blue.

$$\Delta\Delta$$

53. A Touch of Flowers
"Adornment"

The Seeker

The Seeker is sitting in his room, meditating. Sinking deeper into trance, he sees the crown of someone's head beginning to take shape. From his perspective, it is as if he has rotated 90 degrees to his left and is hovering above the head, while looking directly down at its top. The hair is short and tightly curled. Its color initially is jet black. As he watches, its surface begins to shimmer. Where before there was a solid black mass of hair, there is now a field of 6-sided, star-shaped flowers starting to propagate across its curved surface. Each flower is a different color from the ones adjacent to it. All are the same size and shape. Soon the entire head is covered by a jigsaw-like pattern of multi-colored star blossoms. The pointed pedals of each flower are in complete contact with those of all adjacent ones, with no empty space visible between them. Curious as to its texture, the Seeker reaches down with a hand to touch its surface. It still feels like hair to him, having a bristly, spongy like texture to it, reminding the Seeker of how his beard feels. He realizes that he is looking at the head of a magical being, the Vision Dancer of the Fire Ritual.

∆∆

54. The Stranger Self
"Splitting Apart"

The Seeker

The Seeker is sitting in his room in the transitional phase of meditation. Slipping deeper into trance, but still aware of himself and his situation, he sees a face beginning to form. It hovers before him like a face the Seeker would see in a mirror. The individual has grey and white streaked hair, a narrow face, and a predominantly white beard. His demeanor suggests that he is actively looking at the Seeker, trying to determine if he recognizes him. His manner suggests that he does not. This is not the case for the Seeker. He is also actively examining the face before him, but he is doing so precisely because it does look so familiar to him. It finally dawns on the Seeker that what is before him is actually an accurate image of his current self, the very one he sees in a mirror every day, and not the much younger one remembered from his other visions. The Other-Self before him has a different reaction regarding what he is seeing. He looks directly at the Seeker and says, "Who are you? Identify yourself."

Δ

55. The Soul Reversion
"Revolution"

The Seeker

The Seeker is sitting in his room, meditating. Sinking deeper into trance, he is still aware of himself and his situation. A scene begins to form, hovering in space. But rather than appearing in front of him, it takes shape in the area to the left of where he sits. He sees there an image of himself as a young man, the same 35 years of age that he appears as in so many other visions. Both head and upper torso are visible. Suddenly, the image of him starts to pulse and throb, as if some force trapped within was trying to escape. Lines of fracture spread over its surface, which soon shatters into a collection of disjointed polygonal facets. These shapes vibrate and rotate and slide over one another, revealing themselves to be three-dimensional in nature. As he watches, the entire body turns itself inside out, pieces from the inside flowing to the outside, morphing into new shapes and textures as the segments tumble over each other seeking their new destinations. When the transformation is complete, an entirely new person is present. She is a woman, with long straight brown hair, a face that is a softer, feminized version of his original image, still 35 years of age. The Seeker realizes that this woman is the female version of him, and more shockingly, that she is the Teacher.

△△△△

The "Heavenly Revelation" Narrative

The Traveller, transformed, his Soul, revealed as the Teacher,
liberated from the domain of the unconscious and freed from
the grip of the mundane, passes through the Blue Door once
more, climbing up into the Celestial Realm to unlock
the Heavenly Gate and meet the Magister,
where he learns Six Impossible Things,
before returning to Earth, ready to begin
the next stage of his spiritual evolution

NARRATIVE DOMAIN:
FIRE

The Inner Sun Revealed

56. Breath of the Inner Sun
"Nourishing"

The Seeker

Out in the mundane world, the Seeker sits in a Waiting Room, along with several others, who, like him, are patiently waiting to be called into another room for their appointments. Surrounded by plastic chairs and overhead fluorescent lights, the Seeker realizes this is not the ideal place for meditation. Nonetheless, he closes his eyes, orients his body into a relaxed pose, and begins to breath slowly. Following his Practice, he focuses on the shifting amorphous shapes in the dark fields arrayed behind his closed eyelids. In the center of this field, an orange-yellow orb of light begins to form. As he watches, this orb grows in size and morphs into a larger, more diffuse, duller orange-red orb. These two are not really distinct states, but are instead the end points of a continuous and cyclic process of change. This transitioning between bright yellow and dull red states soon becomes a repeating rhythmic cycle, one on which he is able to focus his complete attention without causing any disruption. He soon realizes that the cycles are coordinated with his breathing, bright orange-yellow on the inhalation, and dull orange-red on the exhalation. This pattern seems significant to him. The phenomenon continues without interruption until he opens his eyes.

ΔΔ

57. The Mundane Loses Influence
"Decreasing"

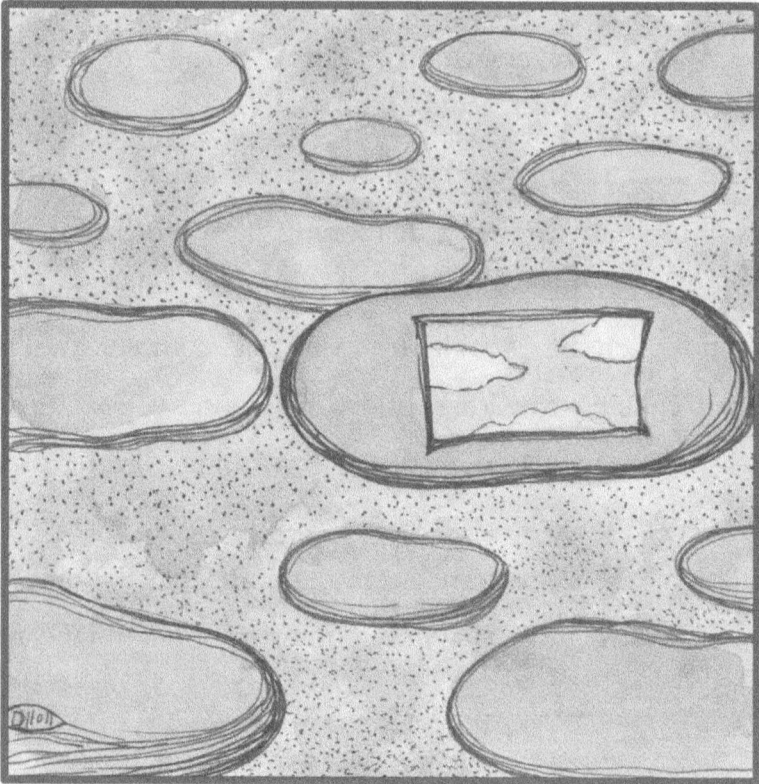

The Seeker

The Seeker is sitting in meditation in the transitional phase, his body numb and his breath slow and gentle. Slipping into deeper trance, he is still aware of himself and his situation. A scene begins to form, hanging in space before him. He is floating above the ground, which is yellow-brown in color and sandy in texture. Covering its surface, he sees a series of grey-blue stones, flattened and smoothed as if burnished by flowing waters in a creek bed. As he watches, the stones begin to wobble and vibrate, the result of some invisible force washing over them. They begin to slide across the ground, colliding and bouncing off each other. Their movements become increasingly more frenetic. Finally, the stones, winning their battle against the forces that constrained them, quiet their frantic motions, and gently rise into the air. There, they settle into slow moving trajectories a couple of feet above the ground, as if they were floating on the surface of a smoothly undulating sea. At this point the Seeker's gaze zooms towards a single stone. He notices some markings on the stone's grey surface. Closer still, he sees a rectangular shaped window set into its rocky surface. Within the window, a bright blue sky is visible, with slowly floating white clouds.

Δ

58. The Yellow Sprout
"Sprouting"

The Seeker

Sitting in shallow trance, the Seeker sees floating before him a patch of barren yellow brown dirt, looking like recent rains have moistened it. He feels himself simultaneously sitting in the chair and hovering above this ground. Everything is quiet and still. As of yet, nothing has grown on this ground. Only small rocks and gravel litter its surface. No life of any kind is visible. Suddenly something begins to stir in the center of this empty region, rising from below and displacing small pieces of earth and gravel, a small eruption of activity. A yellow shoot breaks through its earthen ceiling, turning and undulating, this way and that, as if it were looking around to assess its surroundings. It continues to emerge, snake-like in its appearance and gyrations, wiggling its way out of the confining grip of the clinging soil. As the shoot's movements slow, he gets the feeling that it is looking directly at him. He realizes that this sprout is not plant but a freshly hatched wyrmling, newly emerged into the air. Watching this scene, the Seeker senses a change in the atmosphere, as if some unknown presence had suddenly appeared. Within his mind he hears a voice. "Do not go to heaven." As the vision fades away and he returns to normal consciousness, he is left puzzled and somewhat angered by this utterance.

ΔΔΔΔ

59. Before the Blue Door
"Advance"

The Seeker

The Seeker, in trance, sits in the chair in his room, his Vision-Eyes open. Before him, he sees the familiar bookshelf and other elements lining the front wall, with the room's door to the right, as expected. Suddenly he sees floating at eye level in front of the bookshelf a blue robed, younger version of himself, hair dark and long, face unlined, sitting in full lotus position, with eyes closed. The figure of the Other-Self is clearly deep in a meditative trance. The eyes of the floating figure open and look directly at him. Suddenly the Seeker is now seeing through the Other-Self's eyes, looking back at the now empty chair where he formerly sat. The scene continues to change. The window, which overlooked the pond in the backyard and was set in the wall directly behind and above the chair, has vanished. The wall is solid and now a stark shade of white. Where before there was a blank wall, a door has suddenly appeared. The chair also is gone. The door is solid and unmarked, painted a rich cobalt blue with a silver colored doorknob. The knob begins to turn and the door slowly opens, revealing a glimpse of a lit space behind the wall.

ΔΔ

60. Climbing Heaven's Stairway
"Growing Upward"

The Traveller

The Traveller stands on ground enveloped in a swirling mist, looking at the bottom steps of a stairway that vanishes into the clouds. He knows his task is to climb these stairs. The steps are formed of a pitted granite rock. They are larger than normal size, about two feet deep and high. Beginning to climb the steps, the Traveller soon realizes how steep its ascent is.

Glancing to the side, he is unable to determine the width of the steps, since all he sees is more mist. Step by step he climbs, with the going made increasingly slower by the steep angle and size of each step. Soon he is leaning forward to use his hands and arms to help pull him to the next step. His face drawn close, he notices how worn and corroded the surface is. The mist clears as he rises higher and higher. He now sees that the stairway is built into the side of a giant, multi-leveled pyramid, which grows steeper and steeper the higher it climbs. Climbing still higher, the clouds pull back, and he is able to see a high-walled temple-like structure perched on the top of the pyramid, though it is still far in the distance. He also discovers that he is not alone on the stairway, as he sees a scattering of others struggling up the steps ahead of him, their progress even slower than his as the ascent becomes almost vertical.

Δ

61. Unlocking Heaven's Gate
"Progress"

The Traveller

The Traveller stands upon a broad expanse at the top of an enormous stone block structure that is so large that its lower levels are lost in the clouds. Nor can he, from where he stands, see the top of the structure that looms above him. Alone on the platform, looking down he sees other climbers struggling in vain to make it up the steep steps to where he is standing.

The structure is circled with high walls, dark maroon in color with ornate jade symbols fashioned into its sides. The walls are composed of smooth, ceramic material. Gold trim runs across the wall's top and divides the wall into series of large panels. Walking towards his right in search of an entrance, he comes across two enormous doors. Attached to the wall with golden hinges on their outside edges, the doors are covered with elaborate spiral designs woven of cast iron bars. The doors tower above him. About halfway up he sees a locking mechanism with a slot for a large key. He retrieves the ornate, golden skeleton key that he had strapped to his back. Successfully climbing up the external metal works to reach the panel, he inserts the key and turns it to the right. There is no reaction from the doors, but the key in his hand suddenly disappears. After a short interval his body begins to feel strange. Looking down he sees that his body is growing more and more translucent, dissolving into a mist of golden light.

Δ

62. Visiting the Master
"Great Crossing"

The Traveller

The Traveller walks down a long corridor in a building where everything is painted white. The corridor winds its way through the stark structure, which is laid out more like a labyrinth than the floor plan of a normal building. At first he sees no doors. Finally, the Traveller comes to a section of the corridor in which brown doors begin to sporadically dot the sides of the hallway. Turning a corner, he sees on his left a door that is different from the others. It is blue in color rather than generic brown. It also has a silver colored doorknob instead of bronze. He opens the door to enter a large, richly furnished room, which reminds him of a scholar's study or library. Tall shelves line the walls and an ornate rug sits before a crackling fireplace. Two over-stuffed chairs face the fireplace, which is located on the far wall across from the door. Entering further into the room he sees that one of the chairs is occupied. A well-appointed older gentleman sits there, with grey hair and a white beard, wearing a tweed, three-piece grey suit. He indicates that the Traveller should sit in the empty chair. As the Traveller settles in, the man looks at him and says, "So you're back. You've found me once again." The Traveller nods, though not sure what the man means. He then realizes the man is the Magister he has met before. The Magister pauses and adds, "Very good. I can see that you remember. Shall we begin? I have Six Impossible Things to tell you and your time here is short."

ΔΔΔΔ

63. Soul's Nexus Complete
"Already Across"

The Witness

Floating against a deep black background, the Witness sees a vast field of sparkling, multicolored stars. He soon finds himself in the midst of these objects. Moving closer to them, as they float around him, he sees that they are not stars, but glowing, colored, translucent orbs. He realizes that he has seen these glass-like globes before, though he is not immediately able to remember when or where. He then recalls that these same orbs were on the World Tree of an earlier vision. As he watches, lines of glowing force stream out from all the globes, connecting them immediately with all the adjacent ones, and later with all the others as well. The result is a shimmering, web-like network of crisscrossing lines of energy, with all the globes glowing at the connection points. He is now within this giant mesh network of completely connected nodes. Pulling further back, he sees that the overall network is in the shape of a giant 3-D structure composed of layers of concentric spheres. In the center of this structure he discovers the presence of a golden, sun-like throbbing sphere. He watches as more and more of the surrounding network begins to be pulled towards the central sphere, which grows ever larger as it absorbs their energies. His feels himself starting to move as well, as he is caught up in the space collapsing around him.

$$\Delta\Delta\Delta\Delta$$

64. Descent of the Golden Pearl
"Delight"

The Witness

A diffuse, golden light surrounds the Witness as he hovers within empty, featureless space. He has no sense of body or mass though he feels enclosed within a glowing translucent bubble. He begins to move. The quality of light outside changes, first becoming darker and then gradually lighter, as deep purple gives way to blue. From the direction of the stream of fuzzy shapes he sees passing by, he realizes he is traveling downwards, still wrapped in the golden orb. The sensation of downward movement slows and stops. Dark green shapes hover outside. He begins to move from the center of the glowing mass towards these shapes. Fully outside the sphere, which is left behind him now, he looks out across a meticulously manicured environment. He hovers above a field of close cropped, thick green grass. At the end of the field, sits a row of immaculately groomed hedges. Behind them stand several rows of identical, symmetrically shaped pine trees, each row higher than the last. Rising in height, he recedes away from the trees, until the sphere he traveled in is now a visible part of the landscape. He sees a large golden, glowing orb, pulsing like a miniature, shimmering sun that has come down to earth, hovering above the center of the field. The colors are shimmering and saturated, everything rendered with supranatural sharpness and clarity. The world, like him, is transfigured.

ΔΔ

Afterwards

On Our New Found Destiny:

"We all contain a spark of the divine spirit, which has been embodied within the tomb of living matter and dispersed as soul among our many lives. Our task, over the course of these lives, is to nurture this spark and repair this fragmentation by reintegrating these many lives into a new whole. Only then will we be able to free our true self from the dark confines of matter, to emerge into the full light of wakened consciousness, free to live as creator instead of in bondage to the created."

(From *Hidden Teachings of the Mystic I-Ching*)

What Meditation Has Wrought

Most of us spend our lives secure in the beliefs that this embodied life is the only one we get, that the world we experience within wakened consciousness is the real one and the only one that exists, that we live, in other words, one life in one world. I say "us" because I too had these beliefs.

But then everything changed, not all at once, but rather, turning Hemingway's often-misquoted passage on its head, "Suddenly, then gradually." During an initially intense period lasting three months, and then more slowly over a year and a half, I witnessed a series of extraordinary visionary events, primarily during meditation, that fundamentally overturned my most basic beliefs about life and the world.

I don't make this claim casually, since I have been trained both as a scientist and a philosopher, but I have come to trust the reporting of both my outer and inner senses. Confronted with the full spectrum of all that I experienced, I tried to adopt a more scientific attitude, intending to follow the dictum: "observe and analyze." That is what I have done, in an exercise of what might be called speculative philosophy, in the previous volumes of the *American Tao* series.

As a result of my experiences, my long-held beliefs about the nature of reality and the self have been replaced by a new set of convictions. While my previous books went into much more detail, I end this book by summarizing them here as six main thoughts, which, following Lewis Caroll (and the mysterious Magister of my visions), I call the "Six Impossible Things." Together, these constitute the key elements of a new theory about the meaning of life and the nature of the soul.

The Six Impossible Things

These, in outline form, are the elements of the message conveyed to me by my soul in a series of clues hidden in experiences throughout my life and culminating in the visions described in this book. The idiom of "Six Impossible Things" was brought to my attention by the visionary figure of the Magister (vision #62).

(1)   "You are not your material body and you will not die. But experiences of other lifetimes will only be available to you if your consciousness is open to experiences that are normally suppressed."

(2)   "Neither are you the autonomous and unitary self you thought you were. You are, in your deepest nature, a manifold of other beings simultaneously alive in other places and times."

(3)   "The world in which you spend your waking life is only one of many, existing on parallel planes of being just beyond your own, beginning with the one 'right next door.'"

(4)   "Reincarnation is real, but not in the way you think. Your 'next' life is not always in your historical future, nor even in the same timeline or on the same world."

(5)   "Each life is a step on your evolutionary journey. In order to progress on this path and not stagnate, you have to expand and empower your consciousness by creating psychic connections to your other lives while in this one."

(6) "Your psychic connections to these other lives are established through the energetic channels and gateways of your etheric body, which need to be activated in order to establish more substantial connections."

These new thoughts have transformed my life and if taken to heart, can transform yours as well.

References

Dong, Ming-Dao. *The Living I Ching*. San Francisco, CA: HarperCollins, 2006.

Harner, Michael. *Cave and Cosmos*. Berkeley, CA: North Atlantic Books, 2013.

Huang, Alfred. *The Complete I Ching, The Definitive Translation*. Rochester, VT: Inner Traditions, 2010.

—. *The Numerology of the I Ching*. Rochester, Vermont: Inner Traditions, 2000.

Huang, Kerson, and Rosemary Huang. *I Ching*. New York, New York: Workman Publishing, 1987.

Strasnick, Steven. *Hidden Teachings of the Mystic I-Ching*. Santa Cruz, CA: Mystic Tao Publishing, 2017.

—. *Many Lives, Many Worlds*. Santa Cruz, CA: Mystic Tao Publishing, 2017.

—. *Meditation's Secret Treasure*. Santa Cruz, CA: Mystic Tao Publishing, 2016.

Wilhelm, Richard. *The I Ching or Book of Changes*. Translated by Carl F. Baynes. Princeton: Princeton University Press, 1997.

Also by the Author and Artist

By the Author, Steven Strasnick

Meditation's Secret Treasure. Santa Cruz, CA: Mystic Tao Publishing, 2016

Hidden Teachings of the Mystic I-Ching. Santa Cruz, CA: Mystic Tao Publishing, 2017

Many Lives, Many Worlds. Santa Cruz, CA: Mystic Tao Publishing, 2017

By the Artist, Diana Moll

Assemblage. Santa Cruz, CA: Qi Papers, 2013.

Herb Apothecary: The Coloring Book: 54 Chinese Herbs. Santa Cruz, CA: Qi Papers, 2016.